HOW ANTITRUST
FAILED WORKERS

HOW ANTITRUST FAILED WORKERS

ERIC A. POSNER

OXFORD
UNIVERSITY PRESS

OXFORD
UNIVERSITY PRESS

Oxford University Press is a department of the University of Oxford. It furthers
the University's objective of excellence in research, scholarship, and education
by publishing worldwide. Oxford is a registered trade mark of Oxford University
Press in the UK and certain other countries.

Published in the United States of America by Oxford University Press
198 Madison Avenue, New York, NY 10016, United States of America.

Library of Congress Cataloging-in-Publication Data
Names: Posner, Eric A., 1965– author.
Title: How antitrust failed workers / Eric A. Posner.
Description: New York, NY : Oxford University Press, [2021] |
Includes index.
Identifiers: LCCN 2021017327 | ISBN 9780197507629 (hardback) |
ISBN 9780197507643 (epub) | ISBN 9780197507650
Subjects: LCSH: Antitrust law—Economic aspects—United States. |
Labor economics—United States.
Classification: LCC KF1652 .P67 2021 | DDC 343.7307/21—dc23
LC record available at https://lccn.loc.gov/2021017327

DOI: 10.1093/oso/9780197507629.001.0001

1 3 5 7 9 8 6 4 2

Printed by LSC communications, United States of America

CONTENTS

PART III   Beyond Antitrust

Introduction

IN THE UNITED STATES, and much of the Western world, economic growth has slowed, inequality has risen, and wages have stagnated. Academic research has identified several possible causes, ranging from structural shifts in the economy to public policy failure. One possible cause that has received increasing attention from economists is labor market power, the ability of employers to set wages below workers' marginal revenue product.[1] New evidence suggests that many labor markets around the country are not competitive but instead exhibit considerable market power enjoyed by employers, who use their market power to suppress wages. This phenomenon—the power of employers to suppress wages below the competitive rate—is known among economists as labor monopsony, or simply labor market power. Wage suppression enhances income inequality because it creates a wedge between the incomes of people who work in concentrated and competitive labor markets. Wage suppression also reduces the incomes of workers relative to those of people who live off capital, and the latter are almost uniformly wealthier than the former. Wage suppression also interferes with economic growth since it results in underemployment of labor and, while it may seem to raise the return on capital, actually depresses it, as capital must lie idle to take advantage of monopsony power. With wages artificially suppressed, qualified workers decline to take jobs, and workers may underinvest in skills and schooling. Many workers exit the workforce and rely on government benefits, including disability benefits that have become a hidden welfare system.[2] This in turn costs the government both in lost taxes and in greater expenditures. One estimate finds that monopsony power in the U.S. economy reduces overall output and employment by 13% and labor's share of national output by 22%.[3]

The claim that labor market power raises inequality and reduces growth mirrors another claim that has received attention lately—that the product market power of firms has contributed to rising inequality and faltering growth.[4] A *product market* is a collection of products defined by frequent consumer substitution. When a small number of sellers or one seller of these products exist, we say that each seller has *product market power*, which enables it to charge a price higher than marginal cost, or the price that would prevail in a competitive market. When a small number of employers hire from a pool of workers of a certain skill level within the geographic area in which workers commute, the employers have *labor market power*.

One major source of market power in both types of markets is thus *concentration*, where only a few firms operate in a given market. Imagine, for example, a small town with only a few gas stations. Each gas station sets the price of gas to compete with the prices of the other gas stations. When a gas station lowers its price, it may obtain greater market share from the other gas stations—which increases profits—but it also receives less revenue per sale. If only a single gas station exists, it will maximize profits by charging a high ("monopoly") price because the gains from buyers willing to pay the price exceed the lost revenue from buyers who stay away. If only a few gas stations exist, they might illegally enter a cartel in which they charge an above-market price and divide the profits, or they might informally coordinate, which is generally not illegal, though the social harm is the same. In contrast, if many gas stations compete, prices will be bargained down to the efficient level—the marginal cost—resulting in low prices for consumers and high aggregate output of gasoline.

Labor market concentration creates monopsony (or, if more than one employer, oligopsony, but I use these terms interchangeably) where labor market power is exercised by the buyer rather than (as in the example of gas stations) the seller. Employers are buyers of labor who operate within a labor market. A labor market is a group of jobs (e.g., computer programmers, lawyers, or unskilled workers) within a geographic area where the holders of those jobs could with relative ease switch among the jobs. The geographic area is usually defined by the commuting distance of workers. A labor market is concentrated if only one or a few employers hire from this pool of workers. For example, imagine the gas stations employ specialist maintenance workers who monitor the gas-pumping equipment. If only a few gas stations exist in that area, and no other firms (e.g., oil refineries) hire from this pool of workers, then the labor market is concentrated, and the employers have market power in the labor market. To minimize labor costs, the employers will hold wages down below what the workers would be paid in a competitive labor market—their marginal revenue product. Faced with these low wages, some people qualified to work will refuse to. But the employers gain more from wage savings than they lose in lost output because of the small workforce they employ.

Antitrust law does not distinguish monopoly and monopsony (including labor monopsony): firms that achieve monopolies or monopsonies through anticompetitive behavior violate antitrust law. But product market concentration has received a huge amount of attention by courts, researchers, and regulators, while labor market concentration has received hardly any attention at all.[5] The Department of Justice (DOJ) and Federal Trade Commission's (FTC) Horizontal Merger Guidelines, which are used to screen potential mergers for antitrust violations, provide an elaborate analytic framework for evaluating the product market effects of mergers. Yet, while the Merger Guidelines state that there is no distinction between seller and buyer power,[6] they say nothing about the possible adverse labor market effects of mergers. Similarly, while there are thousands of reported cases involving allegations that firms have illegally cartelized product markets, there are few cases involving allegations of illegally cartelized labor markets.[7]

This historic imbalance between what I will call product market antitrust and labor market antitrust has no basis in economic theory. From an economic standpoint, the dangers to public welfare posed by product market power and labor market power are the same. As Adam Smith recognized, businesses gain in the same way by exploiting product market power and labor market power—enabling them to increase profits by raising prices (in the first case) or by lowering costs (in the second case).[8] For that reason, businesses have the same incentive to obtain product market power and labor market power. Hence the need—in both cases—for an antitrust regime to prevent businesses from obtaining product and labor market power except when there are offsetting social gains.

Why, then, the imbalance between product and labor market antitrust? There are a few possible answers. First, while *economic* theory treats product markets and labor markets similarly, *legal* theory has placed more emphasis on product markets. One possible reason for this is that since the 1960s, legal scholars have influentially argued that the amorphous norms of antitrust law that prevailed earlier in the 20th century should be replaced with a laser-like focus on consumer welfare.[9] The resulting shift in focus naturally favored product market analysis because consumers primarily are injured by price increases caused by product market power. In contrast, primarily workers are injured by the exercise of labor market power. Of course, workers are consumers, and so workers benefited from the law's attention to product markets—but not as much as they would have if the law had paid attention to labor markets as well.

Second, economists until recently assumed that labor markets were approximately competitive, and accordingly that labor market power was not an important social problem. Most people live in urban areas where numerous employers vie for workers. Workers can (and do) move around the country if jobs are scarce or pay is low where they live, putting an upper bound on the social cost of labor market power. A well-known textbook on industrial organization, published in 2005, claimed, "Most labor economists believe there are few monopsonized labor markets in the United States."[10] It is only in recent years that these assumptions have been thrown into doubt. Moreover, academic economics has long been divided into separate fields of industrial organization (IO) and labor economics. IO economists have focused on antitrust problems created by mergers and other corporate actions, while labor economists have focused on labor and employment law. Partly as a result, labor economists never developed the analytic tools relevant to forecasting the impact of increased labor market power that are analogous to or draw on the models IO economists use to analyze product market power.

The DOJ and FTC rely heavily on advice from economists on their staff when evaluating mergers and have frequently challenged mergers based on their effects on product markets. Likely relying on the traditional assumption of economists that labor markets are competitive, the agencies have never blocked a merger because of its effect on labor markets.

Third, antitrust litigation against employers is more difficult than antitrust litigation based on product-market concentration, perhaps giving the illusion that the latter problem is more significant than the former. Product-market litigation is often brought by large firms, which have the resources and incentives to bear the high costs of complex and expensive antitrust litigation. Class actions by consumers are also relatively straightforward because in a typical antitrust case involving product markets, the argument is simply that the consumers paid a higher price than they should have, which means that the consumers share a common interest as required by courts.[11] In contrast, virtually no worker can hope to obtain damages in an antitrust action—even with the treble damages rule—that would compensate her for the cost of litigation. And class actions brought by workers face significant obstacles because workers—unlike consumers—are frequently in diverse positions, defeating the common interest requirement for class certification.[12]

That was the intellectual and legal landscape until a few years ago. The consensus that labor markets were competitive collapsed in response to several events. First, there was the revelation that high-profile Silicon Valley tech firms, including Apple and Google, entered no-poaching agreements, in which they agreed not to solicit each other's employees.[13] This type of horizontal agreement is a clear violation of the antitrust laws. The firms settled with the government, but the casual way in which such major firms, with sophisticated legal staffs, engaged in such a blatant violation of the law alarmed antitrust authorities. The government subsequently issued guidelines to human resources offices warning them that even implicit agreements not to poach competitors' employees were illegal.[14] In 2016 the White House Council of Economic Advisors and the Department of the Treasury issued reports warning of the dangers of cartelized labor markets.[15] The DOJ has also launched criminal investigations of firms for entering no-poaching agreements.

Shortly before this book went to press in 2021, the DOJ announced its first criminal indictments of participants in a pair of wage-fixing and no-poaching conspiracies.

Second, the recent discovery that noncompete agreements—which prevent workers from moving from their employer to a competitor—are extraordinarily common and frequently are applied to low-wage workers raised suspicions that they were being used by employers to exploit their labor market power. For example, Jimmy John's, a sandwich franchise, routinely required low-wage employees to sign covenants not to compete, which apparently deterred those employees from moving to competitors.[16] While these noncompetes were probably unenforceable under the common law, the workers lacked the wherewithal to consult lawyers and threaten (or defend against) lawsuits. The effect was to reduce mobility between jobs, possibly suppressing wages. Researchers subsequently learned that an enormous number of workers—including low-income, relatively unskilled workers—are bound by restrictive covenants. According to one study, in 2014 12% of workers earning less than $40,000 per year with education below the college level were bound by noncompetes.[17] Relatedly, large franchises like McDonald's used no-poaching agreements to reduce competition among franchisees for workers—which in some markets might have resulted in considerable increases in market power.[18] News media reports provide additional anecdotal evidence of the ubiquity of noncompetes and no-poaching agreements and their powerful effect on labor mobility.[19]

Third, economists began investigating monopsony in labor markets. An important spark for this work was a classic study by David Card and Alan Krueger, which found that employment levels were not affected by a minimum wage hike in New Jersey in 1992.[20] While controversial at the time, many other studies of minimum wage increases in other jurisdictions and at other times produced similar results.[21] A possible explanation for the result is that labor markets are monopsonies: if employers pay workers less than their marginal product, then a minimum wage hike—if not too great—will result in higher wages without disemployment.

While other explanations are possible, the monopsony theory gains credence from other studies of the past several years, in which economists, using a range of methodologies as well as previously unavailable sources of data, have found evidence of widespread labor market concentration. I will discuss these studies in chapter 1. The key point for present purposes is that the studies show that most labor markets are highly concentrated and suggest that labor market concentration results in lower wages, as one would expect. In recent years, with the focus on Google, Facebook, and Amazon, people have begun to believe that market concentration is a problem for American consumers. But if market concentration is a problem, it is a bigger problem for workers than for consumers.

***

This book argues that antitrust law should be brought to bear against labor monopsony. I argue that the historical neglect of labor monopsony by antitrust law is not justified by theory, law, or the nature of labor markets. Antitrust law should police labor markets just as it polices product markets. Indeed, the case for antitrust law enforcement in labor markets is stronger than in product markets. Labor markets are likely to be more concentrated than product markets and more vulnerable to anticompetitive behavior by firms. To this end, I lay out the ways in which antitrust law can be adapted to the particularities of labor markets. While I propose some reforms, my main argument is that antitrust law as it is understood today has been underused in labor markets—that good lawyers and sophisticated regulators and judges who are attentive to the special features of labor markets could make progress even without legal reform.

A few words about this book's methodology. Antitrust law is currently embroiled in controversy about its assumptions, goals, and methods. This book does not take sides in this debate. My argument uses the traditional antitrust methods that are currently dominant in courts and academic scholarship. For workers, the problem has not been that antitrust law has the wrong economic goals; it is that antitrust has almost never been applied to labor markets.

And now a word on vocabulary. In antitrust law and IO economics, a firm is a monopoly if it is technically the only seller in a market and, more familiarly, the dominant firm in a market that has multiple firms. While antitrust lawyers and IO economists use the word "monopsony" in a similar way to refer to a single buyer from a product market, in labor economics the term is confusingly used in a more general way to refer to a market in which employers (buyers of labor) pay a wage below the competitive level (the worker's marginal revenue product). Monopsony can be the result of search frictions and other factors. The two groups of economists use the term "market power" in the same way. Product market power means the power to raise prices above the competitive rate; labor market power means the power to pay wages below the competitive rate. Thus, monopsony is a synonym for labor market power, while monopoly is just one source of product market power rather than a synonym for it. I will use the word "monopsony" in both ways: to refer both to a buyer (employer) with labor market power (whatever the source) and to a buyer (employer) who dominates the labor market as a sole or very large employer. Context should keep things clear.

PART I

Labor Monopsony and Antitrust Law

I

Labor Monopsony in the United States

1.1. The Intellectual History of Monopsony

The term "monopsony" was coined by the British economist Joan Robinson in 1933.[1] Before then, economists who wrote about industry structure focused on monopoly and market power in the product market. It had long been clear that large corporations like Standard Oil monopolized goods and services. Robinson realized that corporations also exercised market power on the "buy side"—in their purchases of inputs, including goods, services, and labor. The monopsony power of corporations was just as common as their monopoly power, perhaps more common, but harder to detect.

To be sure, long before Robinson's book, economists and other thinkers understood that employers exercised power over workers. Adam Smith observed that "masters" (employers) tacitly "combined" or agreed not to raise the wages of workers. Anticipating the silence about labor monopsony even today, he wrote:

> We seldom, indeed, hear of this combination, because it is the usual, and one may say, the natural state of things which nobody ever hears of. Masters too sometimes enter into particular combinations to sink the wages of labour even below this rate. These are always conducted with the utmost silence and secrecy, till the moment of execution, and when the workmen yield, as they sometimes do, without resistance, though severely felt by them, they are never heard of by other people.[2]

Later, critics of capitalism like Karl Marx denounced employers' treatment of their workers. They argued that employers exploited their workers by underpaying them, subjecting them to substandard working conditions, and busting unions. Marx argued that employers could keep wages low by taking advantage of what he called the "reserve army of the unemployed."[3] Because people desperately sought work, employers could keep workers' wages below the value of their labor for the employer or for society, at their "labor power" (the minimum they needed to continue working). The extraction of the resulting "surplus value" by the employer was what Marx called "exploitation." Robinson's analysis of monopsonistic labor markets provided a more rigorous formulation of the problem of employer dominance. She pointed out that if labor markets are competitive, employers cannot exploit workers in Marx's sense because workers who are paid only enough to avoid starvation will be able to sell their labor to other employers at a higher wage. Yet labor markets need not be competitive, and when they are not, the outcome for workers is similar to those that Marx identified: excess unemployment, a permanent gap between wages and worker productivity, poor working conditions, and domination of the workers by employers.

Robinson's terminology was adopted by some scholars in the institutionalist tradition in labor economics. For example, in 1946 Lloyd Reynolds, an early founder of the subfield of labor economics, published two noteworthy papers, "The Supply of Labor to the Firm" and "Wage Differences in Local Labor Markets."[4] Both of these papers described empirical features of the labor market (such as wage differences for similar workers within a local labor market) that were consistent with employer market power. Reynolds anticipated virtually all of the modern economic models of monopsony.

While Marx held that the increasing concentration of markets under capitalism would spark a revolutionary transition to communism, and other thinkers hoped that workers would be able to govern themselves in communes and other organizations, the major effect was instead unionization, which, while often militant, was focused on improving wages and conditions for workers rather than overthrowing governments or social orders. In the United States and other Western countries, governments initially resisted the labor movement, often violently, but ultimately accommodated it. Governments passed laws that protected workers from low wages, excessive hours, dangerous workplaces,[5] and other abuses, and that protected labor organization from interference by employers.[6]

The bottom-up nature of worker organization probably accounts for a major bifurcation in the way American policy and law treat the problem of labor market power. While antitrust law, beginning with the Sherman Act of 1890,[7] nominally applied to *all* markets—labor markets as well as product markets—antitrust enforcement would focus almost exclusively on product markets.

Meanwhile, a separate body of law emerged for addressing labor markets. Unions were initially ambivalent toward antitrust law. Union leaders worried that if they made demands on weak employers in a competitive market, the employers would go bankrupt. Better to negotiate with the industry as a whole, and even a single firm that dominated the industry, as long as unions could represent the entire workforce. This ambivalence toward antitrust law turned to hostility when courts initially held that unions themselves could violate the antitrust laws since they combined to fix the price of labor. In 1914, Congress passed the Clayton Act, which exempted unions from antitrust law, but suspicion toward antitrust law lingered. Unions sought and finally obtained—with the National Labor Relations Act of 1935—formal legal recognition by the government and the right to strike and to bargain collectively. Labor organization offered an alternative to antitrust law: rather than break apart employers into competitive buyers of labor, unions bring together workers so that their aggregated bargaining power could counter the bargaining power of the large employer.

This bifurcation of the law led to a bifurcation in economic theory. To address monopolization of product markets, economists developed the field of industrial organization (IO), which seeks to explain how market power affects the structure of business mainly in relation to product markets. To address abuses in the labor market, economists developed the field of labor economics, which focuses on unions and employment regulations. Product markets and labor markets differ in many ways, and economists focused on the most salient aspects of them. IO economists focused on "market structure": why goods and services were supplied in different types of markets, which firms produce the goods and services, and so on. Labor economists focused on training, job mobility, unionization, and related phenomena.

In the United States, the power of unions peaked in the 1950s and has steadily declined ever since. Foreign competition and technological change played a role in the decline of unions. So did the advance of union-busting tactics and rising hostility from business, government, and public opinion. Beginning in the 1970s and accelerating in the 1980s and 1990s, public policy turned against market regulation—both antitrust law and product market regulation, and labor law and labor market regulation. The "neoliberal" revolution reflected frustration with the rigid, outmoded character of traditional market regulation. Yet rather than adapt new laws or organizations better suited to the age of globalization and digitization, reformers focused on dismantling existing market regulation.

1.2. The Sources of Monopsony Power

Economists have identified several sources of labor market power. Because these sources have counterparts in the more familiar analysis of product markets, I will introduce each of them by way of the product market.

In product markets, there are three primary barriers to competition. First, *market concentration* refers to the existence of one or a small number of sellers, usually the result of increasing returns to scale, high fixed costs, or network effects. Second, *product differentiation* exists when goods or services are different from each other rather than fungible; differences across products make comparison difficult, which reduces competition. Third, *search frictions* make it hard for consumers to compare products and seek out the best offering. In both the academic literature and legal adjudication, market concentration typically plays the central role in analysis, with less emphasis on product differentiation and the least emphasis on search. In the literature on labor markets, by contrast, the order of emphasis has been the reverse.

Search frictions. Search frictions or costs refer to the difficulty of finding a job. We all know from experience that finding a new job is not like shopping for clothes or furniture; job hunting requires considerable effort, including research, travel, and interviewing. The problem of search frictions has played the central role in understanding labor markets.[8] In 1998, Kenneth Burdett and Dale Mortensen proposed a model of labor markets with a large number of identical workers and identical firms where search frictions naturally lead employers to have monopsony power.[9] Alan Manning, in his 2003 book *Monopsony in Motion*, presented a wide variety of evidence in favor of what is called the dynamic monopsony model.[10] Because a worker's existing employer knows that the worker's search cost is high, the employer can reduce compensation—including wages, benefits, and workplace amenities— or fail to increase compensation despite the worker's contributions because the employer knows that the worker can find an alternative job only with difficulty.

Job differentiation. In recent years, labor economists have focused on firm-specific amenities of a workplace, which is the labor market correlate to product differentiation.[11] Imagine two workplaces that are identical at an initial point. The employer of each workplace seeks to deter workers from leaving. To do so, the employer might offer an amenity that its workers happen to like—say, a coffee bar or a yoga studio or hot showers. While these amenities may seem frivolous, many of the most important amenities are extremely significant but less apparent as they are "omissions" rather than "commissions"; many jobs involve odd hours and unpleasant or hazardous working conditions. The absence of such "dis-amenities" itself makes jobs attractive. Other amenities might rise more naturally; for example, the location of an employer might appeal to workers because of the convenience to commuting or the attraction of nearby restaurants or other businesses. Differing amenities give rise to search frictions, as noted above, but they separately make it more difficult for workers to compare firms. Indeed, the identities of the other workers at a workplace—whether they are driven and intense, friendly and laid back, or young or old—matter to people, and even very similar-seeming employers, for example, law firms, might be very different in practice. Other common amenities include shift flexibility, childcare, vacation and sick time, and opportunities for promotion and personal growth.

Not only are jobs differentiated along these various dimensions, but workers perceive and value these dimensions differently. Even jobs that seem quite standardized (e.g., cashier) in terms of the productive tasks are frequently valued idiosyncratically by workers who have particular tastes over commutes and workplace relationships. Crucially, firms may not be able to observe this taste heterogeneity. This limitation, plus practical and moral constraints that require firms to post only one wage per job, is what makes labor market power inefficient: if firms could perfectly tailor the wage to each worker's taste for working at that firm, so-called perfect wage discrimination, there could still be market power, but it would not be inefficient, even as all surplus is extracted by the employer.

A major but now forgotten development in labor relations in the United States was the bureaucratization of labor relations, which took place roughly from World War I though the Great Depression.[12] Often at the instigation of the government, which had considerable authority over employers during World War I, employers agreed to regularize work positions. Job categories were defined for the first time; each job category involved specified skills and specified tasks, and workers within each job category received the same pay, adjusted for seniority. Work would take place at certain hours and in certain locations. Job categorization improved efficiency because the publicly stated criteria made it easier to compare and evaluate workers and to transfer them from job to job. Unions supported job categorization because it facilitated bargaining at the level of the bargaining unit; employers would have more difficulty undermining unions by subtly adjusting their pay and conditions of work for workers, creating divisions within the union. Employers were less enthusiastic about job regularization but gave in to pressure from the government and unions and appeared to see some of the benefits of the bureaucratized system. But a key element of job bureaucratization about which employers had no enthusiasm is that it made it easier for employers to compete for workers at other firms since their job category would render workers interchangeable with similar work positions at the poaching firm. The reduction of job differentiation would thus have weakened the employer's labor monopsony.

Employers may have sought to strengthen their labor monopsonies by advancing what was then known as "welfare work," a style of management that took a paternalistic interest in the well-being of workers and their families.[13] The employer sought to create a sense of "family" in the workplace by emphasizing personal ties in the workplace and boosting team spirit with "company picnics, company athletics, company songs, company contests, and company magazines filled with inconsequential gossip about these activities.[14] The economists Samuel Bowles and Herbert Gintis would later emphasize the role of endogenous worker preferences in maintaining employer profits.[15] A large literature in sociology, perhaps beginning with Michael Burawoy's 1979 *Manufacturing Consent: Changes in the Labor Process under Monopoly Capitalism*, argues that employers engineer work environments so as to maximize worker productivity and minimize conflict with management.[16] Workers also develop attachments to coworkers, employers, customers—even the job itself.[17] Employers may try to invest in increasing these attachments by fostering corporate loyalty or specializing the content of training programs.

Labor market concentration. The final and most neglected cause of labor market power is the concentration of labor markets as a result of economies of scale, network effects, fixed costs, and other factors. In many industries a firm with many employees can churn out goods and services more efficiently—at less cost per unit of output—than firms with fewer employees can. Firms can grow large naturally—as they take on additional business and hire workers to supply labor for production or services—or by merging. When a single firm or a small number of firms hire from a labor market, those firms have labor market power. A single firm maximizes profits by choosing a wage below the competitive wage. Since workers cannot quit and find a competing employer to hire them, they must either accept the wage or undergo the costly process of dropping out of the labor market and either retiring or retraining.

When more than a single employer hires from a labor market, but the number of employers remains small (or a few of the employers are dominant while others are minor), employers maximize their profits by paying a wage somewhere between the competitive and monopsony levels. This phenomenon is familiar from the product market. A small number of sellers can engage in parallel pricing or tacit collusion in order to keep prices high. Rather than set prices at marginal costs, they set prices to match those of a price leader (typically the biggest firm) or simply match the prices of their competitors. Employers do the same thing. Large or otherwise salient employers announce wages, and their competitors follow them. Or employers keep wages constant (or adjust them mechanically for cost of living) and raise them only when workers can credibly claim that another employer will pay them more. As long as the number of employers is not too large, they can maintain wages below the competitive rate.[18]

Table 1.1 summarizes the three main sources of labor market power.[19]

While the sources of labor market power are different, their effect is the same.[20] The employer pays a wage below the competitive rate, and employers hire workers at below the competitive quantity. This results in two negative effects for public policy: a loss of output (or efficiency) and a harm to equity if (as is almost always the case) workers are less wealthy than shareholders.

The discussion so far might give the impression that labor markets and product markets are similar: they are both vulnerable to market power (monopsony in the first case, monopoly in the second), and for the same reasons. But there is reason to believe that labor markets are more vulnerable to monopsony than products markets are to monopoly. Labor markets, much more than product markets, are characterized by *matching*.[21] The preferences of *both* sides of the market affect whether a transaction is desirable.

Compare buying a car in the product market and searching for a job. Both are important, high-stakes choices that are taken with care. However, there is a crucial difference. In a car sale, only the buyer cares about the identity, nature, and features of the product in question: the car. The seller cares nothing about the buyer or what the buyer plans to

TABLE 1.1 Sources of Monopsony Power

Sources of monopsony power	Meanings
Search frictions	Workers have difficulty learning about comparable jobs.
Job differentiation	Similar-seeming jobs are actually different because amenities are different, including conditions, commute.
Concentration	Few employers offer a certain kind of job.

do with the car. In employment, the employer cares about the identity and characteristics of the employee, *and* the employee cares about the identity and characteristics of the employer. Complexity runs in both directions rather than in one. Employers search for employees who are not just qualified but who possess skills and personalities that are a good match with the culture and needs of that employer. At the same time, workers look for an employer with a workplace and working conditions that are a good match for their needs, preferences, and family situation. Only when these two sets of preferences and requirements match will a hire be made. This dual set of relevant preferences means that most labor markets are *doubly* differentiated by both the idiosyncratic preferences of employers and those of workers.

These matching frictions both cause and reinforce the typically long-term nature of employment relationships compared to most product purchases, leading to significant lock-in within employment relationships. They are also reinforced by the more geographically constrained nature of labor markets. Products are easily shipped around the country and the world; people are not. While traveling is easier than in the past, and remote work has become more common in the wake of the COVID-19 pandemic, labor markets remain extremely local, while most product markets are regional, national, or even global. Most jobs still require physical proximity to the employer, greatly narrowing the geographic scope of most labor markets, given that many workers are not willing to move away from family to take a job. Two-income families further complicate these issues because each spouse must find a job in the geographic area in which the other can, further narrowing labor markets. Together these factors naturally make workers highly vulnerable to monopsony power, much more vulnerable than most consumers are to monopoly power.

1.3. Measuring Market Power

The economics of labor market power and the harms it causes are closely analogous to the theory of product market monopoly. A monopolist is a firm that does not take market prices as given, but can raise its price, at the cost of some lost sales, to increase the profits it earns on each sale. In choosing an optimal price the firm faces a trade-off.

Raising the price reduces sales but also increases the revenues the firm earns on each unit sold. The higher the firm raises its price, the costlier it is to lose extra demand, as each sale is very profitable. Eventually the firm finds a balance point, where the value of the lost sales from raising the price further just equals the increased profits on the units it sells at the increased price. The firm's absolute markup is the gap between this price and the firm's cost. The markup equals the difference between the monopoly price and the competitive price, and thus serves as a natural gauge of market power.

A similar trade-off between profit-per-unit and number of units sold applies to firms that are not literally monopolists but have some power over their price. In fact, in some sense, every firm with any market power is a "monopolist" over some market, though maybe one too narrow to matter much.

The analysis of monopsony in labor markets is analogous. In a competitive labor market, firms equate the going wage of workers to their "marginal revenue product," the amount of additional revenue the worker can generate. When an employer has a monopsony, it considers the fact that to hire an additional worker it will have to raise the prevailing level of wages for its existing workers and that doing this will increase its overall labor costs. The reason (as noted above) is that employers typically cannot wage-discriminate: they must pay the same wage for the same job. They cannot wage-discriminate because they cannot determine the worker's reservation wage (the wage below which she will quit) and because workers get very angry when they learn that colleagues with the same skill and experience are paid more than they are (known as the pay equity norm).[22]

Conversely, if an employer lowers wages, while it will lose some workers, it will also lower the wage bill on the workers it already employs. As in the monopoly case, a monopsonist will not internalize this effect on workers and will choose a mark*down* of wages below the marginal revenue product. Just as with firms with product market power, an employer with labor market power may not have a "monopsony" over some easily described market, but so long as it will not lose its entire workforce by slightly lowering its wages, it has some labor market power.[23]

Economists use the word "elasticity" to refer to the sensitivity with which one economic variable changes in response to a change in another. "Labor supply elasticity" refers to the sensitivity with which workers react to changes in wages. Suppose that wages across the economy decline a tiny amount, and everyone quits. Then labor supply elasticity is (at the limit) infinity or, in other words, very high. Suppose instead that no one quits; then labor market elasticity is zero. Elasticity can range from zero to infinity. An elasticity of 1 means that if wages increase, say, 1%, then employment will increase 1% as well. An elasticity of 0.5 means that a 1% wage increase will result in a 0.5% employment gain, while an elasticity of 2 means that the same wage increase will result in a 2% employment gain. A relatively high level of elasticity indicating a competitive market for practical or policy purposes might be around 10; the 1% wage increase results in a 10% employment gain. The general view is that labor supply elasticity across the economy is in the neighborhood of 0.5, suggesting a high level of inelasticity.[24] People tend to stay in the workforce even when wages decline below the competitive rate because they need to support themselves.

The term "residual labor supply elasticity" refers to the sensitivity with which workers react to changes in wages at a particular *firm*. Suppose a computer programmer who works at Google would quit and move to Apple if wages at Google decline by a tiny amount. Then the residual labor supply elasticity is high. If the programmer would not quit even if Google lowered wages significantly, then the firm-level elasticity is closer to zero. Like labor supply elasticity (sometimes called "aggregate labor supply elasticity" to distinguish it from "residual labor supply elasticity"), residual labor supply elasticity can fall anywhere along this continuum, though it can never fall below the (aggregate) labor supply elasticity for the relevant category of workers. But it varies greatly from industry to industry.[25]

Residual labor supply elasticity is a simple measure of a firm's labor market power. If workers do not quit even if the firm lowers wages significantly (elasticity is low), then the firm enjoys significant market power over the workers. This is the number that antitrust policy focuses on. If residual labor supply elasticity that a firm faces is high, then the labor market from which a firm draws its workers is competitive, and the firm cannot suppress wages below the competitive wage, or not by much. If it is low, workers need protection.

The economic consequences of labor market power are analogous to those of product market power. Product market power has two well-known effects. It *redistributes* from consumers to the firm: consumers must pay more for products, and the firm earns greater profits at their expense. And it creates *waste* or *deadweight loss*. Some consumers would be willing to pay the efficient, marginal cost price that the firm would have charged in a competitive market but are not willing to pay the higher price the monopolist chooses to charge.

Similarly, monopsony power has two effects. It redistributes from workers to employers by lowering wages. And it creates waste: some workers would have been willing to work for the employer if they had been paid their full marginal revenue product but will quit if they are paid the marked-down wage the monopsonist offers. This leads to increased unemployment or nonemployment as workers find prevailing wages unacceptable and exit the labor force or refuse to take available jobs. Economic output also declines.

Monopsony power creates other negative effects as well. First, to the extent that the degree of monopsony power differs across employers, it will also lead to misemployment: workers may be more productive at employer A, which has a lot of labor market power, than at employer B, which has a little. But B may offer higher wages because of its limited labor market power. The worker may thus choose to work at B, lowering the productivity of the economy. Misallocation may be particularly severe because of the two-sided matching problem. If matches between workers and firms generate specific benefits, monopsony can distort which firms match which workers, which will lower the allocative efficiency of the market.

Second, employers will often cut benefits, rather than cut wages, to take advantage of workers who are locked into the job. The firm has no need to retain these workers and thus may wastefully degrade conditions of work these "stuck" workers particularly value, instead catering only to the workers the firm is worried about losing.[26]

Third, monopsony raises prices for consumers. This may seem counterintuitive: won't lower wages to workers be passed through to consumers as reduced prices? That argument is often made as a defense of monopsony power.

In fact, however, this argument is wrong. To see this, note that if firms employ fewer workers, they will produce less output, resulting in higher prices. The labor cost savings accrue to the employer itself (or its shareholders), not to the buyers of its goods. Those buyers will pay a price that is determined by the structure of the product market, not the labor market. So, for example, if the employer is also a monopolist in the product market, it will charge the buyers the monopoly price—which is determined by how much buyers are willing to pay. And if the product market is competitive, the employer will charge prices for its goods that are no higher than the competitive price—with its competitors taking up the slack as the employer itself will produce less given its small workforce. The technical explanation is that while the firm lowers *wages* to workers, the *cost* to the firm of *hiring* workers rises as the firm now considers the fact that, when it hires an additional worker, it also will pay its other workers more. When a monopsonist hires a single worker, it must increase wages for all its workers. (Recall that employers cannot easily wage-discriminate.)[27] If this seems paradoxical, note that it is merely the flip side of a well-understood feature of monopolistic control of product markets: that a monopolist produces fewer products and charges a higher price for them than does a competitive firm. Monopoly and monopsony are two sides of the same coin, and both harm labor and product markets.

Fourth, and precisely for this reason, monopsony power reinforces and exacerbates monopoly power. In fact, both can be seen as two alternative ways for the owners of capital to squeeze workers and thus reduce the returns to productive work and the output of the economy. The markdown on wages caused by monopsony and the markup on prices caused by monopoly are akin to taxes: payments that ordinary people must pay in order to go about their daily life as producers and consumers. However, the payments go not to governments to fund programs, but to firms and, ultimately, investors. And the payments do not spur investment and raise economic growth because they depend in the first place on the willingness of managers to leave capital idle to obtain market power, while driving workers out of the workforce and onto taxpayer-financed relief programs.

1.4. Evidence of Labor Market Power

Until recently, economists entertained the possibility that labor monopsony could exist, but data limitations prevented any consensus from emerging about its prevalence.[28] The field seemed to conclude that while search frictions could give labor market power to employers, concentration and collusion were not a significant source of labor market power. Historical studies of company towns found weak evidence that they conferred labor market power to employers.[29] Studies of labor markets for nurses found stronger evidence of anticompetitive labor market practices but were vulnerable to methodological objections.[30] There was little doubt that Major League Baseball and other sports leagues engaged in anticompetitive labor market practices, but the unusual nature of these organizations suggested that labor market collusion was anomalous.

Yet there are powerful indications that employers have colluded in labor markets throughout history, often with the help of governments. In England, anticompetitive elements of master and servant law dated back to the 1351 Statute of Labourers.[31] These rules included enticement doctrines, which blocked employers from poaching each other's workers, and criminalization of worker "absconding," i.e., leaving an employer without permission. The feudal legacies may have legitimized anticompetitive practices in labor markets.[32] In the United States, of course, literal ownership of human beings was common in the South until the Civil War put an end to slavery. In the wake of the war and ratification of the 13th Amendment, courts were skittish about enforcing restraints of trade in the labor market. But in the postbellum U.S. South Jim Crow labor law reintroduced anti-enticement rules and in other ways restricted the labor freedom of Blacks.[33] In the North, the labor market power of the trusts was a common source of concern.[34] Nineteenth-century labor activists identified market power of employers as a justification for collective bargaining and regulation, complaining of "wage slavery" and drawing analogies to chattel slavery.[35]

The best data, and hence the best studies, come from the past few decades, and especially the past few years. The evidence consists of studies of many different markets, which tend to show that residual labor market elasticities are extremely low. One should acknowledge at the outset that all such studies face considerable methodological difficulties. The gold standard would be a study in which an employer is somehow persuaded to randomize the wages it offers workers, so that their response could be measured without worries about confounding factors. One group of authors did manage such an experiment and found a (low) residual labor market elasticity of 2.15. But the study involved government workers in Mexico, and hence may not be generalizable to the United States.[36] Convincing firms to randomize their wages in the United States has so far proven hard, and so researchers have relied on a variety of natural experiments and indirect observations to estimate the extent of labor market power.[37]

An early finding that stimulated the development of monopsony as a candidate model of the labor market for low-skill labor was the evidence on minimum wage effects produced by David Card and Alan Krueger.[38] Conventional wisdom in the economic profession at the time held that minimum wage laws will reduce employment, based on the assumption that low-skill workers are normally paid a competitive wage. In a given market, for example, a city, there are many employers who are willing to hire low-skill workers—including custodial workers, security guards, sandwich makers, and the like. The multiplicity of possible employment opportunities should minimize the labor market power of any employer. If so, then employers pay workers a wage equal to their marginal product, and an employer who is forced by law to raise wages would have to fire any workers whose marginal product is below the legal minimum or lose money. However, Card and Krueger found no such wage effect, suggesting that workers were paid less than their marginal product, and hence the employer could absorb the higher wage rate. Numerous studies have attempted to replicate the Card and Krueger result, too many to discuss here. But many studies found evidence consistent with Card and Krueger's. For example, Arindrajit Dube, Suresh Naidu, and Michael Reich found that the San Francisco minimum wage law of 2007 raised wages without lowering employment, and lowered turnover.[39] Recent work by Dube, Reich, and T. William Lechter expands the analysis to the entire U.S. labor market and finds that minimum wage laws increase wages without reducing overall employment.[40] Other papers, using a variety of methodologies and data sets, find that workers are surprisingly insensitive to wages, failing to quit when wages are pushed down.[41]

Another way to assess monopsony is to estimate the effects of labor market concentration on wages. This is, of course, of considerable importance for antitrust law, which focuses on market concentration. The labor market is often defined by commuting distance for a given occupation. Alan Manning and Barbara Petrongolo estimate a model on job application data from the U.K. to look at application behavior of workers and find that workers' application rates to a job are quite sensitive to distance, suggesting that labor markets are quite local.[42] Ioana Marinescu and Roland Rathelot also find high sensitivity of applications to distance in U.S. data, with application rates falling by 35% for jobs 10 miles away from a worker's residence.[43]

José Azar and his coauthors find substantial labor market concentration in labor markets throughout the United States,[44] a finding confirmed by another near-contemporaneous study performed using a different data source.[45] The studies measure concentration using the Herfindahl-Hirschman Index (HHI). We will discuss the HHI in greater detail later; for now, understand that the HHI ranges from 0 (the theoretical ideal of perfect competition) to 10,000 (a single firm— a monopolist or monopsonist). The U.S. government believes that market concentration becomes an antitrust problem as the HHI passes 1,500, and alarm bells go off when it reached 2,500. (HHI of 2,500 can represent different combinations of firm numbers and sizes, including, for example, four firms with equal 25% market shares.) Figure 1.1, taken from the Azar paper, depicts average labor market concentration across the United States at the county level.

As the figure shows, labor market concentration is pervasive. Alarming HHIs greater than 2,500 prevail in 60% of labor markets, while astronomical HHIs greater than 7,200 prevail in a quarter of labor markets. The reason is obvious once one thinks about it. Most of the United States is thinly populated. In rural and suburban areas, the population can support a Walmart, a few fast-food joints and gas stations, and perhaps a chicken-processing facility, manufacturing plant, or farm. An accountant or lawyer will not find many employment opportunities in such areas. Even in more densely populated parts of the country, many jobs are so specialized that only a few employers need people to work

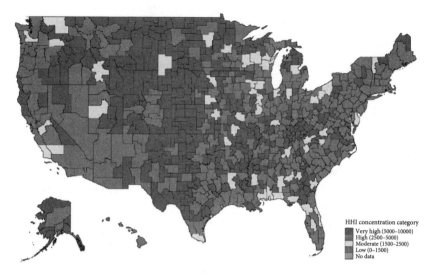

FIGURE 1.1. Average HHI by commuting zone, based on vacancy shares.

Note: This figure shows the average of the HHI by commuting zone code for the top 200 SOC-6 (Standard Occupational Classifications used by the federal government, at the six-digit level) occupations (ranked based on the number of vacancies) over the period 2016-Q1–2016-Q4 in the Burning Glass Technologies data set.

for them. And because many people cannot move much because of family ties and local connections, they cannot seek out better employment opportunities in the big cities.

Studies are rapidly accumulating,[46] and by the time this book is published, many of the results I have discussed will be superseded. Indeed, as this book goes to press, a new study by Berger, Herkenhoff, and Mongey introduces a novel general equilibrium model of monopsonistic competition that can replicate many of these empirical studies, but adds further complications to the picture.[47] The authors show that for a given level of concentration, welfare losses due to labor market power can be larger if larger employers are more productive, which is the case in the data. Their paper suggests that looking at concentration alone can severely understate the welfare losses from labor market power, which suggests even richer tests might be needed. But there is little doubt that the traditional model of competitive labor markets is wrong, that monopsony or monopsonistic competition is pervasive, that many labor markets are highly concentrated, and that labor monopsony, as theory would predict, pushes wages below the competitive rate.

1.5. Implications for Wages and Employment

What, concretely, do these findings suggest about wages, employment, and other features of the labor market? Overall, the recent evidence suggests that low labor elasticities, ranging from 0.1 to 5.5, are common throughout the economy. Even the residual supply of low-skill labor is relatively inelastic, in the range of 1 to 3, despite the earlier conventional wisdom that inelastic labor markets were caused by the time and cost of obtaining education and specialized training, which low-skill workers, by definition, lack.

Residual labor market elasticities from 0.1 to 5.5 correspond to deadweight loss ranging from 60.5% down to 7.9%, and a labor share ranging from 8% to 65%. Thus, even if one takes a conservative approach and believes the studies with weaker findings, it remains clear that monopsony causes considerable harm both to the economy and to workers. Imagine a market where firms face a residual labor elasticity of 100. The harm to the economy is only 0.5% and arguably no longer a matter for public concern. If a worker with a marginal revenue product of $50,000 is employed by a firm facing elasticity of 100, she will be paid $49,504.95. If the elasticity is 3, she will be paid $37,500. If the elasticity is 0.1, she will be paid $4,545.45 (at least in theory). It is plausible, then, that in many labor markets, workers are paid at least several thousand dollars per year below the competitive rate.

In other work,[48] Suresh Naidu, Glen Weyl, and I conducted a few simple calibrations of the efficiency and distributional consequences of a variety of levels of labor market power for the entire economy. The assumptions and calculations are tedious; the interested reader may consult the original source. The graph in Figure 1.2 shows our results. As the degree of monopsony increases from 0 to maximal (the horizontal axis, moving from left to right), labor's share of economic output declines from over 70% to around 20%—generating increasing losses in income per capita, tax revenue, and employment.

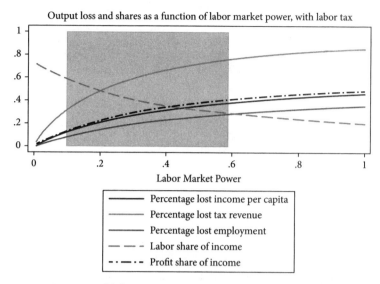

Output loss and shares as a function of labor market power, with labor tax

Labor Market Power

——— Percentage lost income per capita
——— Percentage lost tax revenue
——— Percentage lost employment
— — - Labor share of income
-·—·- Profit share of income

FIGURE 1.2 Impact of labor monopsony on economic outcomes.

The shaded area shows the range of the studies we relied on for our parameters, thus giving a sense of what they imply about the impact of plausible levels of labor monopsony on income, profits, output, and tax revenue. Within particular markets, where workers are vulnerable because of their lack of skills, or because of specific constraints they face on mobility addressing labor market power is extremely urgent.

2

The Failure of Antitrust

IF LABOR MONOPSONY IS a problem, then antitrust law should be the solution. It is the body of law that addresses problems of market competition and market structure. Yet antitrust has played almost no role in addressing labor monopsony and instead has allowed it to fester. This chapter offers some insights into this mystery.

2.1. Background on Antitrust Law

The antitrust laws prohibit firms from cartelizing markets and from creating monopolies except when the monopolies arise naturally from innovation and natural features of the market. Section 1 of the Sherman Act prohibits contracts "in restraint of trade."[1] Section 2 of the same law prohibits attempts to "monopolize . . . any part of the trade or commerce among the several States."[2] The Clayton Act prohibits various practices associated with the exercise of market power, including price discrimination and—of special interest to us—mergers and asset acquisitions where "the effect of such [merger or] acquisition may be substantially to lessen competition, or tend to create a monopoly."[3]

The unusually broad language of the antitrust laws has been given specific meaning by the courts over many decades of judicial development. Today, courts and most commentators agree that the purpose of the law is to prevent firms from obtaining market power except as a result of innovation and other practices that generate social benefits. Otherwise, market power results in distortions that cause social harm.

A monopolist or a cartel will raise prices by restricting production; the reduction in output is a social harm. A labor monopsonist or labor cartel will lower wages by reducing hiring, and the reduction in hiring means lower output, the same social harm. Monopoly and monopsony produce other social harms as well, including redistribution from poor to rich and others that we will see in due course.

The vast majority of cases have involved efforts to block sellers from cartelizing or monopolizing product markets. However, the law and the cases are not limited to anticompetitive behavior by sellers. The courts have recognized that buyers can engage in anticompetitive behavior. When all the sellers in a market sell to a single buyer, the buyer is said to have a monopsony. When only a few buyers exist, an oligopsony exists, and the buyers violate the antitrust laws if they conspire to suppress prices by agreeing not to compete for products sold by sellers in the market. Because the statutes do not distinguish sell-side and buy-side anticompetitive behavior, and buy-side anticompetitive behavior produces the same type of harm as sell-side anticompetitive behavior, the Supreme Court and other courts have not hesitated to recognize that the antitrust laws apply to both types of behavior.[4]

Most monopsony cases involve allegations that buyers have tried to monopsonize or cartelize markets for goods and services. Consider, for example, a big retailer like Walmart, which may possess the buy-side market power to suppress the prices that it pays to wholesalers. A handful of such cases involve buyers who have tried to monopsonize or cartelize the labor market. Again, nothing in the antitrust laws distinguishes labor markets from other types of market, and the courts have agreed that anticompetitive behavior in labor markets violates the antitrust law. The partial exception is Section 6 of the Clayton Act, which provides that workers do not violate antitrust laws when they organize unions—a form of labor cartel, at least in the economic sense.[5] But Section 6 does not immunize an employer from antitrust liability if that employer attempts to suppress competition in the labor markets.

However, antitrust litigation based on anticompetitive behavior by employers in labor markets has historically been quite rare. One can find old cases in England and the United States where no-poaching agreements and related combinations were held to be restraints of trade, but these cases are few and far between.[6] The remedy at the time was generally nonenforcement of the agreement rather than monetary damages, which are normally required to finance a lawsuit; workers were vulnerable to retaliation if they brought lawsuits then as now. After the Sherman Act was passed by Congress, the pace of labor monopsony litigation barely advanced. In the earliest cases, *employers* brought suit against workers for organizing unions—and frequently won, as unions are in form price- (wage-) fixing conspiracies, though the drafters of the Sherman Act did not have unions in mind when they drew up the law. Section 6 of the Clayton Act put an end to this legal theory, and the National Labor Relations Act of 1935 would recognize the lawfulness of labor organization. Meanwhile, in 1926 the Supreme Court finally recognized that employers could violate antitrust law by fixing wages.[7]

Unions might have been a vehicle for private enforcement of antitrust law. They had the resources and sophistication. But, burned by the earlier use of antitrust law against them, they seemed to fear that if they brought antitrust lawsuits against employers who combined against them, they would legitimize and strengthen a weapon that might boomerang. Moreover, antitrust law remained a threat for unions in certain contexts where unions tried to use their power beyond the normal boundaries of organization, negotiation, and the calling of strikes.

That has left workers to fend for themselves, occasionally with the help of entrepreneurial attorneys who take advantage of the class action. In a handful of cases, employees have challenged cartel-like arrangements under Section 1 of the Sherman Act, arguing that employers have fixed wages or taken other actions to suppress competition among themselves for labor. The most prominent cases have involved hospitals, which have been accused of coordinating pay scales for doctors and nurses, and sports leagues like Major League Baseball and the National Collegiate Athletic Association,[8] where employers could not avoid publicizing the rules that restricted competition for players.

Antitrust challenges relating to labor markets have never gone beyond the most overt type of cartelization among rival employers. The Horizontal Merger Guidelines focus almost entirely on the risk of product market concentration and say nothing about the risks of labor market concentration.[9] The DOJ and FTC have *never* challenged a merger because of its possible anticompetitive effects on labor markets, or even rigorously analyzed the labor market effects of mergers as they do for product market effects. (Shortly before this book went to press, the FTC—apparently for the first time ever—issued an analysis of the labor market impact of a proposed hospital merger in Texas, arguing that the merger would result in excessive concentration of the labor market for registered nurses.)[10] Nor have I found a reported case in which a court held that a merger resulted in illegal labor market concentration.[11]

The infrequency and rather unusual nature of antitrust litigation involving labor markets for a long time seemed to verify (though it really was founded on) economists' assumption that labor markets are normally competitive. But the erosion of this assumption in recent years—driven, as noted earlier, by the consolidation of employers, the noncompete scandal, and empirical evidence of wage stagnation and labor market concentration—has been accompanied by significantly greater legal and regulatory activity.

In 2010, the Justice Department entered a settlement with major high-tech firms—including Apple, Google, and Amazon—over their no-poaching agreements, which prevented them from hiring away one another's employees.[12] The DOJ and FTC also issued a guidance document informing firms that it is illegal to enter into such agreements.[13] In 2014, the Jimmy John's noncompetes scandal broke. The scandal led the White House and Department of the Treasury to issue reports criticizing overuse of noncompete agreements, while many state legislatures have considered bills and passed laws restricting noncompete agreements involving low-wage workers.[14] The White House report also noted evidence of labor market concentration, warranting stricter enforcement of antitrust laws against employers. Litigation has been commenced against McDonald's and other firms that use no-poaching agreements within franchises.[15] The Justice Department has begun criminal investigations of employers suspected of entering no-poaching agreements.[16]

Meanwhile, over the past half-century, a wave of industry consolidation has given employers greater bargaining power in labor markets. This industry consolidation, which began in the 1970s,[17] was hardly a secret, but commentators focused on the possible effects on product markets, not labor markets. For example, commentators worried that mergers in the airline industry, which reduced the number of major American airlines operating in the United States from more than 10 in the 1980s to four today,[18] might raise ticket prices for consumers, but not that it might suppress the wages of pilots, flight attendants, and airline mechanics. Hospital consolidation has raised concerns about the creation of monopsony conditions for nurses and physicians, especially in small towns and rural areas.[19] Consolidation has taken place in many less salient industries as well, where working conditions are harsh and wages are low. For example, the meat-packing industry has gone through a series of mergers.[20] Because many food-processing establishments are in remote, rural areas where labor markets are concentrated, the effect of mergers on wages in this industry could be significant. Consolidation has also taken place in sectors of great importance for labor markets, including the freelance services industry[21] and the temporary staffing industry.

2.2. The Litigation Gap

Labor monopsony cases are rare, but a natural response is "Compared to what?" A starting point for thinking about labor market litigation is product market litigation. Labor market litigation is certainly rare compared to product market litigation, as Figure 2.1 shows.

What accounts for this litigation gap? A number of possibilities suggest themselves.

Theory. One possible argument is that as a matter of economic theory, firms have a stronger incentive to seek control over product markets, which allows them to raise prices, than labor markets. The litigation gap exists just because firms do not monopsonize as much as they monopolize. However, the two types of incentives are symmetrical. A firm that controls labor markets increases profits by reducing labor costs, while a firm that controls product markets increases profits by raising prices. The effect on the bottom line is the same.

The empirical prevalence of monopolized markets. Another theory is that product markets are more numerous than labor markets or that product markets are more concentrated than labor markets are. However, there is no reason to think that product markets are more numerous than labor markets. There are many nationwide product

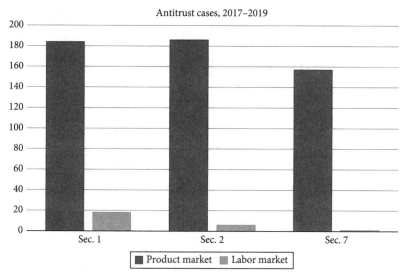

FIGURE 2.1. The Litigation Gap

Note: Section 1 and 2 counts are based on searches of the antitrust database in Westlaw (based on Westlaw searches for "section /3 1 /3 sherman +1 act & product +1 market"; "section /3 1 /3 sherman +1 act & labor +1 market"; "section /3 2 /3 sherman +1 act & product +1 market"; "section /3 2 /3 sherman +1 act & labor +1 market" [January 15, 2020]). Section 7 counts (for labor markets, the number is zero) are taken from the DOJ and FTC (U.S. Dep't of Justice Antitrust Division and F.T.C., Hart-Scott-Rodino Annual Report, Fiscal Year 2019, available at https://www.ftc.gov/system/files/documents/reports/federal-trade-commission-bureau-competition-department-justice-antitrust-division-hart-scott-rodino/p110014hsrannualreportfy2019_0.pdf).

markets, involving commodities like oil, goods like cars, and so on, and very few nationwide labor markets.[22] That said, there are also many local product markets, and I have not found anyone who has bothered to count them up. For labor markets, a rough estimate based on the product of commuting zones and job classifications suggests as many as 267,546 labor markets; if we count only labor markets with at least 100 employed workers, then this number falls to a still high 173,653. Sixty percent of the labor markets in the top 200 occupations (representing 90% of all vacancies)—more than 70,000—are highly concentrated, and more than 8 million people work in those markets.[23] Even if product markets outnumber labor markets, we would surely expect more than a handful of labor market cases.

With respect to comparative market concentration, labor markets are probably more concentrated than product markets are because they tend to be more local. As noted in chapter 1, 60% of U.S. labor markets have an HHI above 2,500; 25% of labor markets have an HHI above 7,200.[24] We do not have comparable figures for all product markets, but if we focus on manufacturing in 2012, product market HHI is 411 on average, compared to 3,955 for the labor market HHI weighted by local employment.[25] Most workers may be able to find jobs in labor markets with only four or five employers. Consumers, by contrast, frequently face dozens of choices among the manufactured goods they buy.

Conventional (but dated) wisdom in economics, and data limitations. A third theory is that lawyers have brought relatively few labor market cases because economists have told them that labor markets are usually competitive, and, until recently, the statistical evidence of labor market monopsony has been limited. Indeed, much of the evidence has become available only in the past several years. In contrast, evidence of concentration in product markets has been available for quite some time. Economic advances in understanding product markets have been driven forward by product market litigation, which has financed it, in a self-reinforcing cycle. Because so little labor-side litigation has taken place, research on labor monopsony has lagged.

Postwar economists assumed that labor markets were reasonably competitive, and accordingly that labor market power was not an important social problem. Indeed, by the 1970s, if not earlier, economists had begun to see unions, not employers, as the major threat to labor market competition. In contrast, then, labor markets that were not unionized were seen as idylls of competition. Most people (including economists and lawyers) live in urban areas where numerous employers vie for workers. Workers can (and do) move around the country if jobs are scarce or pay is low where they live, putting an upper bound on the social cost of labor market power even if it exists.

Legal hostility/uncertainty. The scarcity of labor monopsony litigation has left behind a thin trail of case law. Another self-reinforcing cycle may be at work. Because there is more product-side litigation than labor-side litigation, there is more product-side case law, and thus product-side outcomes are easier to predict. Because lawyers understand product-side law better than labor-side law, they are more likely to bring product-side cases, which further develops product-side law.

Courts have struggled with labor monopsony cases. As we will see in later chapters, they often make basic errors, not even realizing that labor markets are different from product markets.[26] Misled by the mirror-image analogy of product-market analysis, they conduct the labor analysis backward.[27] In nearly all the cases I have found, the labor market definition is superficial. Plaintiffs fail to describe the geographic limits of the labor market,[28] do not distinguish different labor markets within a class,[29] fail to defend their labor market definitions,[30] and so on. In other cases, the courts have rejected reasonable market definitions because they assume that labor markets are broader than they in fact are.[31] Finally, a few of the cases are difficult to explain as anything other than judicial skepticism, or at least uncertainty about how to address arguments in the absence of well-developed case law.[32]

Government neglect. A large portion of private product-side litigation piggybacks on government investigations and litigation, which both uncover otherwise unknown antitrust violations and establish useful precedents.[33] The near absence of government enforcement of antitrust law in labor markets until very recently thus helps explain the scarcity of private litigation. Even today, the government's attitude toward labor monopsony claims reflects a degree of skepticism. Early in 2019, the DOJ filed notices in several class actions in which it argued that the franchise no-poaching agreements being challenged should be evaluated under the more onerous rule of reason rather than the per se rule.[34] While the Justice Department's argument is not absurd from a legal perspective, the application of the rule of reason makes private litigation harder in practice, thereby cementing monopsony power. The government's interventions in private litigation signal skepticism toward these claims.

The DOJ and FTC rely heavily on advice from economists on their staff when evaluating mergers and have frequently challenged mergers based on their effects on product markets.[35] Relying, I suspect, on the traditional assumption of economists that labor markets are competitive, the agencies have never blocked a merger because of its effect on labor markets—or even, as far as I know, given the labor market effects of a potential merger more than cursory attention. Nor does it appear that the agencies have employed labor economists who might have drawn the agencies' attention to the possible effects of mergers on labor markets—though, in any event, because labor economists have until recently given this topic little attention, they would have been of little help even if they had been consulted.

Class actions: incentives and law. Private litigation against monopolists takes two forms: class actions and litigation brought by corporate rivals or victims. Class actions are financed by lawyers, and so are risky and expensive. In the case of product markets, however, class actions are often nationwide—because product markets are often nationwide—and thus offer potentially enormous damages.[36] In contrast, the classes in labor market cases are usually small, involving a geographically limited group, often those living in a town or city, and hence a lower level of damages.[37] Lawyers who specialize in antitrust law naturally given more attention to product-side class actions with national markets.

Moreover, employees may have more trouble with class certification than consumers and other product-side victims do. In a consumer-side class action, plaintiffs usually allege that the defendant has charged a supracompetitive price.[38] Class members are thus similarly situated: they bought the same goods, and all paid a price higher than they should have. Subtle variations—for example, volume discounts or price changes—can be handled algorithmically. In contrast, employees who bring labor-side cases typically differ from each other along numerous dimensions. One court, in denying a motion for class certification, noted:

> The types of injury Plaintiff alleges are (1) decreased salaries and (2) deprivation of new job opportunities. In order to prove these types of injury, a number of individual determinations would have to be made. Defendants point out that resolution of each claim would depend on the consideration of several factors; for example, whether the employee's contract was the result of arms length negotiation, whether a covenant not to compete was included in a particular employee's contract; the employee's salary history, educational and other qualifications; the employer's place of business; the employee's willingness to relocate to a distant competitor, and their ability to

seek employment in other industries in which their skills could be utilized (e.g., pharmaceuticals, cosmetics).[39]

Other antirust plaintiffs have had more luck.[40] And outside of antitrust law, courts have been more willing to certify classes of workers.[41] But the broader point stands. Because products are simpler and more homogeneous than workers, product-side class actions will be more common than labor-side class actions.

Lack of information. Class action lawyers face another incentive to focus on product markets. Consumer prices are public information, and price increases frequently receive public attention.[42] Sellers may try to disguise price increases by reducing quality—for example, selling cereal in smaller boxes, offering more limited warranties for consumer electronics, increasing waiting times for consumer support, or breaking promises to protect data. But these quality variations also attract public attention, as consumers complain and the media catch on. Consumer class actions can also piggyback on earlier lawsuits brought by rivals who successfully complain that an antitrust defendant has illegally cartelized the market. Those plaintiffs sue to recover profits or dismantle anticompetitive arrangements, but they leave in their wake information that can be used by class action lawyers to prove that consumers were harmed as well. In contrast, most employers keep aggregate wage information confidential, and while individual workers may report their wages to the media or to lawyers, the variations across an entire workforce can more easily be kept secret with nondisclosure agreements and other legal instruments. Yet without this information, lawyers cannot bring claims.[43]

Arbitration clauses and the absence of natural corporate plaintiffs. A further problem for both consumer and employee class actions is that firms frequently use arbitration clauses to block class action litigation. The Supreme Court has validated this practice for antitrust claims.[44] However, these clauses cannot be used to block litigation brought by well-funded corporations that are not in privity with the firm in question, and hence antitrust cases brought by corporate plaintiffs can continue. These cases compose a large fraction of product-side litigation. But there are few such cases on the labor side.[45] A possible explanation is related to the small size of most labor markets. If a firm tries to raise entry barriers by tying up the local labor supply with noncompetes and other arrangements, then the plaintiff who sues that firm is likely to be itself a small firm. A large firm, such as a manufacturer, can locate factories elsewhere and thus is not constrained to compete in the local market. A firm that needs a local labor force to serve a local market will often be relatively small.

It might be thought that unions would take up the slack and bring cases on behalf of their members. This has indeed happened. But unions are wary of antitrust law. Unions are themselves cartels of workers. In the early years of antitrust law, firms sued unions for violating the antitrust law and often won. While in 1914 Congress enacted the labor exemption, which protects unions from antitrust challenges, there are still ways that unions can run afoul of antitrust law if they are not careful. In light of the historical legacy along with continuing litigation risk, unions remain small players in the drama of antitrust.

Labor and employment law. The traditional legal approach to protecting workers, which took place "outside" antitrust law, may have seemed sufficient. This traditional legal approach had two branches: labor law and employment law. Labor law protected workers who sought to form unions to combat the market power of employers. The theory was that if workers banded together, they could use legally mandated collective bargaining and the threat of strikes to prevent employers from paying them monopsony wages. Employment law granted workers specific protections: minimum wages, maximum hours, safe workplaces, privacy rights, and the like. Employment law countered employer labor market power by preventing employers from granting workers wages and benefits below a somewhat artificial floor. It may well be that lawyers, judges, and economists, seeing that these areas of law address the problems of workers' lack of market power, saw antitrust law as irrelevant to this problem. However, both types of legal protection have eroded over the years. Union activity has collapsed in the United States because of deregulation, foreign competition, aggressive anti-union tactics by employers, and a chilly legal environment.[46] The federal minimum wage law has eroded through inflation; other employment protections are vulnerable to the vagaries of budget-setting and enforcement priorities among the relevant agencies.

And all these worker protection laws assume traditional employment practices, which are rapidly being replaced by independent contractor arrangements, outsourcing, and other practices of the "gig economy."[47]

***

The antitrust litigation gap has not been filled with other legal protections for workers. But even if those legal protections were introduced, a role remains for antitrust law. Labor markets, like product markets, are best for society when they are competitive. In part II, I propose ways for strengthening antitrust law so it can more adequately address labor monopsony.

PART II
Reform

3

Collusion

FIRMS COLLUDE TO FIX prices, and they collude to fix wages as well. While long ago courts gained a handle on the first set of cases, they often fumble labor cases. The 2019 case of *Llacua v. Western Range Association*[1] offers an example. A large group of foreigner workers entered the United States with agricultural work visas to work as sheep herders on ranches throughout the United States. They had been recruited by two organizations that had been established by owners of those ranches. According to the complaint, the ranchers authorized the organizations to offer wages, which the organizations fixed at the minimum allowable by law. If a group of sellers established an organization to jointly offer their goods to buyers for a common price, that would be price fixing accomplished through the offices of an agent. But the 10th Circuit Court of Appeals rejected the plaintiffs' antitrust claim.

The court's main argument was that the complaint failed to allege facts from "which it can be inferred ranches needed to offer more [than the legal minimum wage] to attract a sufficient number of qualified workers."[2] Moreover, the conspiracy "made no economic sense" because the ranchers had "no rational economic motive" to "depress wages paid by their competitors in other states."[3] This is like saying that producers would never enter into a price-fixing conspiracy because the conspiracy benefits rivals as well as themselves. Price-fixing conspiracies make economic sense because all of the conspirators gain—and the same is true for wage-fixing conspiracies. Competitors are supposed to bid against each other so that they end up charging customers less than those customers are willing to pay and workers more than the workers are willing to work for. That is the essence of the market system that antitrust law protects.[4]

To understand why the court went wrong, and what to do about it, I start in this chapter with a brief discussion of how product-market cases are evaluated under Section 1 of the Sherman Act. Then I discuss the labor-market setting, and close with some suggestions for reform.

3.1. The Law

Product markets. Under Section 1, firms are prohibited from entering agreements that have an anticompetitive effect. Some agreements are presumptively ("per se") illegal because they are likely to stifle competition.[5] Most price-fixing agreements are per se illegal because they prevent price competition, though there are some cases where price fixing may be necessary for the goods to be produced.[6] Agreements to divide a market geographically or to limit competition over customers are also per se illegal. However, most agreements are more complex and require a "rule of reason" analysis, where the court must determine that the conspirators possess sufficient market power to be able to restrain competition, that they actually do restrain competition, and that the agreement lacks a procompetitive justification. Vertical restraints of trade—agreements between parties at different locations on the distribution chain—are subject to rule of reason analysis. Because the parties to the agreement do not compete, the agreement is not obviously anticompetitive, and so then the question becomes whether the agreement enables one party (or both parties) to block competition from its (or their) competitors.

Courts routinely adjudicate Section 1 product market cases. A Westlaw search suggests about 50 cases per year.[7] Defendants include the largest and most important corporations in the United States. Many of the cases involve blatant antitrust violations (some of which resulted in criminal prosecution), where top executives met secretly to set prices or carve up product or geographic markets. A huge number of cases involve more subtle scenarios, where, for example, competitors exchange pricing information, conduct joint ventures, participate in trade associations, and agree with upstream suppliers or downstream buyers to limit resale, control quality, refuse to deal with competitors, and so on.

Labor markets. Section 1 applies to agreements to restrain competition in labor markets in the same way as it applies to product markets. Collusion can take many forms that mirror the types of collusion one finds in product markets: agreements to fix wages; to refrain from poaching (that is, hiring away) each other's employees; to hire from different geographic areas; to hire different types of people; and to exchange wage information in order to coordinate wage rates. Plaintiffs benefit from the per se rule for wage-fixing agreements and other simple agreements that mirror the product-market-side agreements covered by the per se rule.[8] Otherwise, plaintiffs have been forced to contend with the rule of reason. They must show that the defendants enjoy market power sufficient to restrain labor market competition and that the agreement hinders rather than advances competition.

Courts rarely adjudicate Section 1 labor market cases. A Westlaw search suggests about six cases per year, about a tenth of the results for product market cases.[9] And about half of these cases involve the special setting of sports leagues.[10] In the sports league cases, a league or similar organization—the National Football League, the National Collegiate Athletic Association—coordinates various businesses that operate teams that compete against each other. The league agreement may restrict competition in multiple ways, for example, by regulating how much the teams pay players; in the NCAA case, the teams pay the players nothing.[11] Courts use rule of reason analysis to distinguish restrictions that are necessary to ensure that league play is possible and those that merely suppress compensation for athletes.

The remaining cases are more straightforward lawsuits against competitors in a particular industry who are accused of holding down wages. In *Fleischman v. Albany Medical Center*,[12] for example, registered nurses accused hospitals in the Albany area of agreeing to suppress wages for these employees. There are a handful of other such cases, mainly in the hospital industry.[13]

An instructive case is *Todd v. Exxon*,[14] which shows the barriers facing plaintiffs who seek relief from monopsony. Employees of 14 oil and petrochemical companies alleged that the companies exchanged salary information for nonunion managerial, professional, and technical

(MPT) employees in the industry as a part of a conspiracy to suppress wages. The plaintiffs argued that the companies, which jointly employed 80%–90% of these employees, used the information to determine wages. The plaintiff provided statistical evidence that one of the defendants, Exxon, reduced pay over the relevant time period while keeping it in line with its competitors.

The district court dismissed the case for several reasons. First, it said that the plaintiff failed to plausibly define what it called the "product market"—it meant the labor market—because the employees are not "reasonably interchangeable."[15] Second, it believed that the relevant labor market must encompass every industry in which the MPT employees could obtain jobs—not just the oil industry—and thus the actual market share of the defendants was much less than 80%–90%. Third, the court held that the claim depended on the possibility of tacit coordination, but this was impossible because the market was not concentrated. It added that the plaintiffs had also failed to show that "demand for these 'products' is inelastic."[16] Fourth, it argued that Exxon's wage-setting behavior could have been unilateral rather than pursuant to agreement, and hence the plaintiff had failed to allege an agreement that could survive a motion to dismiss.

The court (or possibly the lawyers who represented the plaintiff class, or everyone) was seriously confused. While it is true that the plaintiff lumped together different types of employees—lawyers and engineers, for example—each occupation could certainly be a labor market. Moreover, an MPT labor market (or group of labor markets) limited to the oil industry could exist if, as the plaintiffs alleged, there were special characteristics of that industry that required experience and training to master, as is likely the case. The court's reference to demand inelasticity was also inapposite: the question was whether the supply of labor was inelastic in the sense that if wages were reduced in the claimed labor market(s), employees would have refrained from finding work elsewhere. Finally, the claim did not depend on agreement to suppress wages but agreement to share information, which was clearly alleged.[17] The question whether the agreement to share information affected wages was a matter for trial. The court of appeals, in an opinion by then-Judge Sotomayor, reversed on roughly these grounds, though it too incorrectly referred to the labor market as a product market (probably because the plaintiffs did as well).[18]

While the court of appeals rode to the rescue, the district court's opinion suggests some reasons why this type of case is so rare. The district judge clearly held a widespread—but incorrect—belief that labor markets are competitive and that employees are not normally confined to a particular industry. Thus, he found reasonable allegations to be implausible. He also tripped over the product-side analogies and, as a result, made a hash of the economics of the plaintiff's claim.

Plaintiffs have enjoyed more success with lawsuits against employers who have entered no-poaching agreements—agreements not to hire away each other's employees. In 2010, the government sued the Silicon Valley tech firms for entering no-poaching agreements, which the firms settled.[19] Piggyback litigation was also successful.[20] Plaintiffs were helped by the egregiousness of the firms' behavior: express promises by the tech companies' CEOs not to solicit each other's employees.[21]

The Silicon Valley case was notable because of the prominence of the firms involved, including Apple and Google. It is unclear whether the CEOs who orchestrated the agreements were oblivious or contemptuous of antitrust law. Concerned that firms were simply unaware that antitrust law applies to labor markets (or, more likely, aware that antitrust law was hardly ever enforced against employers), the U.S. government trumpeted its settlement with the tech firms and later circulated a guidance to human resources departments that warned them off no-poaching agreements.[22]

It was right to do so. Around the same time another no-poaching agreement involving prominent institutions had been negotiated. The case arose when a radiologist at the Duke University School of Medicine applied for a position at the University of North Carolina–Chapel Hill School of Medicine, which was located a half-hour's drive away. The relevant department head at UNC initially expressed great enthusiasm. But later he wrote, "I agree that you would be a great fit for our cardiothoracic imaging division. Unfortunately, I just received confirmation today from the Dean's office that lateral moves of faculty between Duke and UNC are not permitted. There is reasoning for this 'guideline' which was agreed upon between the deans of UNC and Duke a few years back. I hope you understand."[23] In a subsequent email, he explained, "[T]he 'guideline' was generated in response to an attempted recruitment by Duke a couple of years ago of the entire UNC bone marrow transplant team; UNC had to generate a large retention package to keep the team intact."[24]

Needless to say, the defendants settled with the plaintiffs and the U.S. government, which had intervened. Here again, top officials at highly respected institutions agreed not to poach each other's talent. But for an errant statement in an email, the conspiracy might never have come to light.

Claims in more complex cases, in which agreements not to recruit are, for example, ancillary to settlements or other transactions, have been less successful.[25] In *Eichorn v. AT&T*,[26] AT&T sold one of its subsidiaries to another company, and as part of the transaction agreed not to hire or solicit any of the more highly compensated employees of that subsidiary for eight months. The employees sued, arguing that the no-poaching agreement violated Section 1. The court evaluated the transaction under the rule of reason standard because the agreement was ancillary to the sale of the company, and held in favor of the defendants. A crucial part of its analysis was its rejection of the plaintiffs' market definition, which was "potential employers within a 35 mile radius of Holmdel/Middletown with the capacity and capability of employing or utilizing large numbers of persons with specialized experience in high speed data communications equipment of the sort Paradyne [the subsidiary] develops and makes."[27] The court said that the market definition should "[include] all those technology companies and network services providers who actively compete for employees with the skills and training possessed by plaintiffs."[28] It added that "there are over twenty companies that compete for employees with plaintiffs' technical skills. Additionally there are a 'vast number of jobs' nationwide for plaintiffs with more generalized work and educational experience."[29] With such a broad market definition, AT&T lacked market power. But this market definition is too broad. Most workers do not move far away to find new jobs,[30] and when specialized skills are not transferable, the employer exercises market power.

Courts have also stumbled in cases involving no-poaching agreements within franchises. Some old doctrine suggests that franchises should be treated as a "single entity"; therefore, no-poaching agreements imposed by the franchisor on franchisees cannot be a violation of Section 1 as there cannot be a one-party "agreement."[31] More recently, the Supreme Court has recognized that the single entity doctrine honors a legal fiction,[32] one that allows firms to collude to suppress wages, and has been taken advantage of by many franchises.[33] An entrepreneur can choose to profit by setting up a franchise (like McDonald's) or by operating through a single company (like Walmart). The advantage of the franchise form lies precisely in the independent nature of the businesses, which enables the entrepreneur (established as the franchisor) to avoid the risk of labor organization against the entire operation, and in most cases liability for wrongdoing committed by the franchisees. Yet even today courts sometimes absolve franchises of antitrust liability under the single entity doctrine.[34]

3.2. Is Labor Market Collusion Different from Product Market Collusion?

Identifying collusion in labor markets is more difficult than doing so in product markets, for several reasons. First, the compensation received by workers is often confidential, while prices for goods and services are nearly always public. And even when salaries or wages are public, the compensation paid to workers is often more complicated than the compensation paid to sellers. In the case of workers, an employer might nominally pay the same wages to all but give some workers more time off than others, or more autonomy, or access to more amenities, or more shift flexibility. In contrast, products (and services as well) are often commodified—that is, identical regardless of who purchases them. Finally, because workers typically spend a long period of time with a single employer, the nature of their labor and their effective compensation will diverge over time, based on their talents and the employer's needs. An employer may offer flexibility and benefits to longtime, loyal workers that are not available to new workers; there is no analogy to this in product markets except loyalty programs, which are available for a limited number of products and services. If the effective compensation of workers is hidden or partly hidden and complex, plaintiffs will have trouble establishing that employers suppress compensation through collusion.

Second, employers exercise power over their workers and have information about them to an extent that has no parallel in product markets. If an employer's workers begin to quit at an increasing rate, the employer can quickly figure out why. Supervisors, former colleagues, the workers themselves, and records left behind by departing workers may reveal why the workers quit—whether they quit to work for a competitor, for example, or for some other reason. The workers who remain are a captive audience, eight hours a day, for the employer's efforts to explain why they should not leave. And if the employer knows where the workers depart for—a specific competitor, for example—it can arrange a deal with that competitor to restrict mobility. In product markets, sellers can employ expensive market surveys to understand why their customers have left for competitors, but they have neither the means nor the information that employers have, and thus are in a weaker position to approach competitors for collusive purposes.

Third, as we have seen, labor markets are more concentrated than product markets; they are also more local. That means that in many labor markets, bosses are few and likely to know each other and to congregate in clubs and professional associations. Where product markets are competitive, or relatively so, the opportunities for sellers to collude are fewer and more liable to detection by authorities. And even when they are not, product markets are, unlike labor markets, frequently national or regional, which means the opportunities for collusion may be fewer and more complex to arrange.

Fourth, labor markets are sociologically rich in ways that product markets are not and in ways that give employers advantages relative to sellers. The pay equity norm is powerful in labor markets, and this means that employers can engage in only limited wage discrimination. By contrast, while customers sometimes complain when they learn that they were charged higher prices than others, the principle that sellers can price-discriminate is relatively established; people experience this principle in action all the time, for example, when they buy airplane seats. Wage and price discrimination reduces the deadweight cost of market power. If price discrimination is easier than wage discrimination, then product markets will be more efficient than labor markets even if the degree of concentration is the same. Employers are also in a better position to build up loyalty than sellers are, which in turn reinforces the employer's power to suppress wages below the competitive rate.

The first of these factors—the greater difficulty of obtaining wage information than price information—is nicely illustrated by a recent case against food-processing companies. The case was brought by a class of workers who labored in chicken-processing plants owned by Perdue, Tyson, and other major food-processing companies.[35] The complaint alleges that the defendants exchanged information about the wages of these poorly paid workers, agreed to fix them, and monitored compliance with the various agreements they made with each other over a long period of time. As the complaint explains, because chicken-processing plants cluster in the areas in which chickens are raised by farmers, multiple plants are found in relatively small areas in which they compete for workers. If the allegations in the complaint are proved in court, the plaintiffs should have a remedy under Section 1.

Perdue, Tyson, and the other chicken-processing companies have also been sued for *price* fixing.[36] The two cases have factual overlap: in both cases, plaintiffs argue that the defendants exchanged information through various intermediaries, including a company called Agri Stats. From a certain jaundiced economic perspective, it is not surprising that large firms should attempt to fix prices—nor that they have been sued for doing so, whether or not the claims turn out to be meritorious. That same perspective suggests that firms should fix wages as well, and yet the wage-fixing claim comes much later and seems much more surprising.

Yet it is also easy to see why the price-fixing case came first. The chicken-processing firms are enormous companies whose actions are followed by analysts and reported in the media. In 2010, after much disruption in the industry, a number of firms cut production, resulting in price increases. Normally, one would expect other firms to increase production in order to seize market share and reap profits, but that did not happen. Instead, production remained low and prices continued to increase. All of the information that was needed to establish this pattern was public, including details about the closing of facilities, production numbers, and prices. A number of suspicious public communications and meetings was enough to get the plaintiffs beyond a motion to dismiss, enabling them to use discovery to advance their case.

In contrast, similarly useful public information about wages and workforces was not available—not at a sufficiently fine-grained level, which would disaggregate with respect to types of workers, their location and job category, seniority, types of compensation, and so on. Workers would not know that their wages are suppressed; class-action lawyers would have no indication of anticompetitive behavior. It seems likely that the second wage-fixing lawsuit was made possible only by the revelation in the course of discovery during the first lawsuit that the agencies used to share price information were used to share wage information as well. And yet the harm caused to workers was far more focused and damaging than the harm caused to consumers, which was diffused through a massive population.

3.3. Parallelism

Black letter law says that plaintiffs cannot advance a claim against antitrust defendants based on mere "parallelism" or "conscious parallelism."[37] Parallelism occurs when two or more competitors maintain above-competitive prices by (for example) adopting pricing strategies of matching the other party's price. They keep prices high through unilateral behavior rather than through agreement. Many commentators have criticized this legal rule because it allows firms to engage in anticompetitive conduct that hurts buyers.[38] The Supreme Court, however, has adamantly resisted calls for reform. The problem, first identified by Donald Turner, is that there is no clear judicially manageable remedy for parallelism.[39] A court could issue an injunction requiring the defendants not to engage in parallel pricing, but it would be hard to determine whether they are or not. It is in the nature of pricing that the seller must pay attention to the prices of other sellers, and a court would normally be unable to determine what the competitive price is. By contrast, if an agreement exists, the court can enjoin it and punish the parties for entering the agreement.

A similar point could be made about parallel wage setting. Imagine that one firm announces the wages that it pays its workers, and other firms match the wage. Workers at one or all the firms sue, arguing that the firms coordinate to keep wages low. A court might have difficulty fashioning a remedy for the same reason as in the case of parallel pricing: it may be impossible for the court to determine whether a firm ignores or pays attention to the wages of other firms and to issue an enforceable order directing the defendants to ignore them.

Support for this worry comes from Jeremy Bulow and Jonathan Levin's analysis of the National Resident Matching Program, which is used to match medical school graduates with residency positions in hospitals.[40] The authors demonstrate that a public promise by an employer that it will not engage in wage discrimination—that salaries will be "lockstep" based on objective indicators like seniority—undermines competition for workers and lowers wages. If all employers know that their competitors will not pay a worker a wage above the lockstep rate, then the employers can more easily collude on wage levels, knowing that if they refuse a higher wage to a particular employee, they need not worry that a competitor will lure away the employer with a higher wage. If antitrust law denies a remedy, then employers are free to suppress wages.

But Turner's objections do not apply in all settings. Consider, for example, another common form of parallel behavior: nonpoaching. Firm A does not hire from Firm B, and Firm B does not hire from Firm A. It is likely that if Firm A and Firm B both employ large workforces and frequently hire people, a plaintiff could establish with statistical methods that Firm A turns down qualified applicants from Firm B—that is, applicants who are as qualified as the applicants from outside Firm B that Firm A hires. An antitrust violation thus could be established, and an appropriate remedy—based on the but-for world in which Firm A uses the same standards for all applicants—could be formulated. The same tools that are used to show invidious discrimination in a disparate impact employment discrimination case could be used in the antitrust context.[41]

For an example, consider *Kelsey K. v. NFL Enterprises LLC*,[42] where the court rejected both a no-poaching and a wage-setting allegation based on parallel conduct. The plaintiffs, a class of cheerleaders, tried to establish the no-poaching allegation by pointing out that no NFL team had ever hired a cheerleader away from another team even though the skills employed by cheerleaders are easily transferred from one team to another. The court held that the refusal to hire could have been merely parallel conduct; an agreement was not necessary. The court should have taken the no-poaching allegation more seriously. The problem of proof and remedy in the price-setting and possibly wage-setting context was not present in this case. If cheerleaders routinely applied for positions at other clubs and were routinely refused, this should be a prima facie case of a Section 1 violation. The teams could defend themselves by showing that they had applied the same employment criteria to applicants who belonged to other clubs and applicants who did not.

An employer can rebut a disparate impact claim by showing, using statistical methods, that the low representation of a group in its labor force reflects demographic constraints, for example, the low representation of that group in the labor market from which the employer draws.[43] When a plaintiff claims parallel or reciprocal no-poaching, the employer would similarly be able to rebut the claim by showing that its labor force has the same proportion of former employees from the plaintiff's employer as from other employers, controlling for other variables.

A flat ban on labor-side antitrust cases brought on the basis of parallel practices is unwise. Courts should recognize Section 1 cases based on parallelism when statistical analysis shows that the parallel behavior harms labor competition. The greater risk of collusion in labor markets because of their high level of concentration justifies relaxed standards for Section 1 in labor market cases because the risk of false positives— wrongfully imposed antitrust liability—is correspondingly lower than in Section 1 product market cases.

3.4. No-Poaching Agreements in Franchises

In the past few years, plaintiffs have brought class actions on behalf of workers at franchises like McDonald's and Jimmy John's, arguing that these franchises have used no-poaching agreements in order to suppress competition.[44] The McDonald's no-poaching agreement reads:

> *Interference With Employment Relations of Others.* During the term of this Franchise, Franchisee shall not employ or seek to employ any person who is at the time employed by McDonald's, any of its subsidiaries, or by any person who is at the time operating a McDonald's restaurant or otherwise induce, directly or indirectly,

such person to leave such employment. This paragraph . . . shall not be violated if such person has left the employ of any of the foregoing parties for a period in excess of six (6) months.[45]

A franchise that violates this provision is subject to a range of sanctions from McDonald's, including termination if repeated violations occur.[46] In the McDonald's case, the class representative, Leinani Deslandes, alleges that she was employed by a McDonald's franchise in a managerial position for $12 per hour.[47] After her original employer frustrated her efforts to obtain training for a higher-level position, she applied for a managerial job at a nearby McDonald's restaurant that offered $13.75 per hour, rising to $14.75 after three months. The store manager expressed interest in Deslandes's application, but she was later told by a McDonald's official that the store could not hire her without the consent of her original employer, who refused it because she was "too valuable."[48] She eventually quit and went to work for Hobby Lobby for $10.25 per hour, the lower wage reflecting the fact that "some of the skills [Deslandes] developed as a manager of a McDonald's outlet were not transferable to management positions at employers outside of the McDonald's brand, so she had to start over at the bottom elsewhere."[49]

The franchise cases raise several novel issues for antitrust law. First, when the franchisor imposes within-franchise no-hire obligations on the franchisees, do these obligations count as vertical agreements or horizontal agreements? If they are vertical agreements, then they are subject to the rule-of-reason standard, which favors the franchise. If they are horizontal agreements, they are presumptively subject to the per se standard, which favors the employees. Antitrust policy reflects deep skepticism of agreements between competitors, while agreements among firms in different positions on a distribution chain may produce efficiencies. In the Jimmy John's case, the court seized on the contractual right of franchisees to sue each other for violating the no-poaching obligation, which has a horizontal feel.[50] Unfortunately, the distinction between horizontal agreements and vertical agreements is hopelessly tangled. The type of formalism employed by the Jimmy John's court will simply cause firms to rewrite the franchise contract so that the franchisor alone enforces the obligations.

Second, does it matter that these agreements are "intrabrand," that is, between firms that are contractually bound by the franchise agreement rather than between independent firms? In product market cases, agreements that restrict trade within a brand are not subject to per se analysis because they can facilitate competition across brands.[51] If McDonald's owned all its restaurants rather than contracted with franchisees, then it would be impossible to argue that restrictions on employee mobility would violate the antitrust laws, which do not apply internally to the operation of a firm.[52] Why should matters change if McDonald's operates through franchises? One possibility is that unions can more easily organize against a single large firm than multiple independent franchises; thus, it might seem fair that if McDonald's can counter unionization by organizing itself as a franchise, it should be subject to antitrust law. But it seems that one cannot answer this question without examining the market conditions in which McDonald's operates.

Third, and getting closer to these economic realities, one needs to ask whether these no-poaching obligations are likely to be pro- or anticompetitive. The McDonald's court made several pertinent observations. The McDonald's no-poaching agreement applied to low-skill workers as well as managerial workers, and it applied to workers whose training took place in the distant past as well as workers whose training was recent.[53] The no-poaching clause was not tailored to the presumed business justification: to protect each restaurant's investment in its employees' training. Moreover, "[g]iven that most individuals in the low-skill employment market do not have the luxury of being unemployed by choice for six months, the no-hire provision effectively prevented competing McDonald's franchises (as well as the company-owned stores) from competing for experienced, low-skill employees."[54]

McDonald's could insist that Deslandes show that the labor market was concentrated because if it were not, Deslandes could have found an equally good job. The low Hobby Lobby wage might have shown that she did not look hard enough or that she valued other amenities at Hobby Lobby more than the lost income. As a first step in refuting this argument, Deslandes would need to show that the labor market was concentrated. While this would not necessarily be difficult, the court noted that "allegations of a large number of geographically-small relevant markets might cut against class certification."[55] And if a class cannot be certified, we can be sure that Deslandes's claim, however meritorious, will never be vindicated. Even trebled, $2.75 per hour in damages will not finance a single expert report on market conditions.

No-poaching agreements for low-skill workers are almost certainly socially harmful. Employers invest little in low-skill workers and probably can depend on ordinary labor market frictions to protect the investments they do make. Meanwhile, the workers—poorly paid, vulnerable, and unlikely to have access to legal counsel—are harmed, and production is reduced.

Thus, the law may be inadequate to the job of policing labor market conditions. There are a few strategies for addressing this problem. First, courts should allow plaintiffs to bring class actions based on the general practices and policies of franchise systems while allowing them to flexibly define subclasses that reflect local labor market conditions. This would address the class certification problem noted by the McDonald's court. I will discuss labor market areas in greater detail in the next chapter. Second, courts should keep an eye out, as the McDonald's court did, for no-poaching obligations in franchise contracts that are untailored to the skill level and responsibility of employees or that apply to low-skill employees. Within-franchise no-poaching obligations may be justified in narrow cases, for example, involving managerial employees who are given access to proprietary information about the franchise's method of business or who have received intensive training at the franchise level; when the obligations apply to nonmanagerial employees, they should be automatically ("per se" in antitrust jargon) illegal. This approach would be more fruitful than the tangle over vertical versus horizontal restrictions.[56]

3.5. Vertical Agreements

A classic vertical conspiracy is resale price maintenance. A supplier, normally a monopolist, sells goods to distributors and requires the distributors to resell the goods above a stipulated price. This conspiracy reduces competition among distributors, who might otherwise reduce their markup in order to obtain a larger share of the retail market. The supplier and the distributors can share the rents obtained through the conspiracy.

Labor-side analogies are easy to imagine. Indeed, some lawsuits against Uber have this flavor. Uber supplies a platform to drivers, and then controls the prices that the drivers charge customers. If Uber has monopoly power over (technically) the market for driver-passenger-matching technology,[57] then it can further generate market rents by blocking competition among drivers.[58] To see why, imagine that Uber's platform matched drivers and passengers but allowed drivers to compete for passengers by offering different fares over the app. The drivers would compete fares down to the competitive level. Uber would be able to charge a monopoly price to drivers, which would be incorporated into the fare, but the drivers themselves would not be able to charge a markup above the cost of inputs because of their competition among themselves. Uber puts a stop to this competition by preventing drivers from competing with each other, and it can take a large cut of these monopoly rents (that is, the markup the drivers are required to charge).

Or consider vertical collusion with nonprice terms. Imagine an employer who hires workers and requires them to agree to a long-term contract—of several years, say. If the workers breach the contract, they must pay a high level of liquidated damages; moreover, a noncompete clause blocks them from working for competitors. It is easy to see that a large employer could lock in a large portion of the labor market, preventing other firms from entering the labor market and obtaining enough workers to offer competition to the incumbent employer. An antitrust case against such an employer would be difficult to win because long-term employment contracts may have efficiency benefits. But there does seem to be a substantial risk that provisions like these can be exploited by labor monopsonists. I will explore these themes in greater detail in subsequent chapters.

4

Monopsony

SECTION 2 OF THE Sherman Act prohibits firms from acquiring or maintaining monopolies by engaging in anticompetitive actions. The law was passed under the shadow of the trusts of the Gilded Age, and the law's most famous triumphs came against the great monopolists: Standard Oil, AT&T, Microsoft. In recent decades, significant victories under Section 2 have been rare, but uneasiness with the tech industry has spurred a new round of government investigations of and private cases against Silicon Valley behemoths, including Google, Apple, and Facebook. In contrast, there has been as yet no interest in suing employers for illegal monopsony under Section 2.

This is not because employer monopsony is rare. According to one study, 25% of labor markets have an HHI above 7,200,[1] implying a dominant firm with market power above 80%. Even if this figure turns out to be a significant overestimate, thousands of employer monopsonists exist in the United States. These monopsonists are less visible than the tech firms or the historic trusts because they are mostly local. They include meat-processing plants in rural areas, superstores or giant warehouses in depressed towns, and firms that own chains of dentists' offices or physical therapy practices. A few national firms—like Walmart or Amazon—might be local monopsonists in various labor markets, but most local monopsonists have names that most people have not heard of.

Monopsony, like monopoly, is not regarded as bad in itself by law and policy. If Amazon opens a warehouse in a depressed local community and seizes a large market share in a relevant job category, it will initially benefit residents, not hurt them. The trouble comes if Amazon, once ensconced in the area, uses its labor market power to block new entrants or extend its power into other markets. Even though Amazon benefits workers initially, over time it may pay them less than their marginal revenue product. The challenge for the law is to prevent Amazon from underpaying workers and blocking rivals while not discouraging it from entering the market in the first place.

4.1. The Law

Section 2 prohibits firms from obtaining or maintaining monopolies through anticompetitive means rather than "naturally" or in pro-competitive ways, for example, through innovation.[2] A typical Section 2 case involves a defendant who already monopolizes a product market and is accused of using its monopoly power to block other firms from entering the market or to extend its monopoly power into new markets. The plaintiff must normally define a product market, establish that the defendant controls a large share of that market, and prove that the defendant obtained or maintained that monopoly in an illegitimate way.

Section 2 product-market cases are adjudicated almost as frequently as Section 1 product-market cases—about 60 to 70 per year.[3] But they can be hard to win because allegedly anticompetitive behavior can frequently be given a business justification. For example, while a monopolist that gives discounts to buyers who commit to buy a large volume of its products could be accused of trying to maintain its monopoly by depriving market entrants of demand, it might also be cheaper to sell to large-volume buyers than to small-volume buyers. Monopolists who are accused of extending their monopolies to new markets can argue that they are offering buyers in one market the convenience of transacting with the same seller in another market. Still, there have been many notable Section 2 cases, including the government's case against Microsoft, which monopolized the market for operating systems for IBM-clone personal computers.[4]

Plaintiffs should similarly be able to bring Section 2 cases against employers who monopsonize labor markets. Plaintiffs need to define a labor market, establish that the employer controls a large share of the labor market, and prove that the employer has obtained or maintained that monopsony by engaging in anticompetitive acts. However, Section 2 labor monopsony cases are extremely rare. A Westlaw search yielded only two cases in the past year and six cases over the past three years.[5]

The results of the Westlaw search probably understates the problem. I have not found a single Section 2 labor monopsony case, ever, in which the claim survived a summary judgment motion. And nearly all the cases I have found are ones in which the Section 2 claim is tacked on to a more substantive claim, such as a Section 1 collusion claim or a non-antitrust claim relating to a garden-variety employment-law dispute. In most of these cases, the plaintiff failed to define a labor market or to defend the labor market definition or failed to identify an anticompetitive act. In other cases, the plaintiff lacked standing.

A few examples illuminate the dismal landscape. In *Thomsen v. Western Electric Co.*,[6] employees of Western Electric sued that company, its parent AT&T, and another subsidiary, Pacific Telephone, for violating the antitrust laws by agreeing not to hire each other's employees. On the Section 2 issue, the court held that employees lacked antitrust injury because they accused the defendants of monopolizing the product market (telephone service) rather than the labor market, which they should have identified and defined as craft telephone workers in the relevant geographic market.[7] The court's view is reasonable: a firm that monopolizes the product market harms consumers but does not necessarily harm workers; indeed, the workers might benefit if managers decide to share the monopoly profits with them, and in any event will not be harmed if the labor market is competitive. Thus, there is no antitrust injury.[8] The Section 2 claim also failed because a company's internal policy not to allow employees to move among its divisions did not reduce competition as understood in antitrust policy, which encourages independent employers to compete with each other for workers but does not require intrafirm competition.[9] Thus, even if the employees had properly defined a labor market, they might still have lost.

In *Minnesota Association of Nurse Anesthetists v. Unity Hosp.*,[10] a group of anesthesia nurses sued hospitals that had "outsourced" them—fired them and then rehired them through various intermediaries that directly employed them. The nurses' main argument was that their terminations were the result of a conspiracy between anesthesia doctors, who sought to eliminate competition from the lower-paid nurses, and the hospitals, who passed on the increased cost to Medicare. The court wrongly held that to show antitrust injury the nurses must show that anesthesia prices would increase, which they could not—but in any event, the nurses apparently did not try to show that their compensation declined.[11] On the Section 2 claim, the nurses argued that the hospitals conspired to push down their wages. But the court rejected the claim because neither hospital controlled a substantial portion of the anesthesia market—though the court should have looked at the labor market for anesthesia nurses, not the product market for anesthesia services.[12]

4.2. What Is a Labor Market?

In virtually every Section 2 case, the plaintiff must define the market in which the defendant operates. (In other types of antitrust cases, including Section 1 cases and merger cases, market definition also may play a role.) For a labor monopsony case, the plaintiff must define the labor market that the defendant dominates. A labor market is technically defined in terms of the substitutability of the services provided by people who are hired by employers. As a practical matter, in both economic research and legal analysis, a labor market is defined by the type of job and a geographic area.

Job type. First, we define a labor market by the type of job. The academic literature relies on a list of Standard Occupational Classifications (SOC) maintained by the Bureau of Labor Statistics,[13] and more specifically an occupation at the six-digit SOC level, which represents a fairly specific definition of a job or occupation. Unfortunately, even the detailed six-digit SOC level is probably too broad for labor market definition. For example, "accountants and auditors" (13-2011) may be excessively broad because an experienced accountant may consider only a "senior accountant" job title position rather than the position of a junior or entry-level accountant.[14] The SOC will provide a starting point for antitrust analysis, but only that.

Antitrust law typically uses the hypothetical monopolist test to determine the scope of a market. If the question is whether product X counts as a market, the answer is no if consumers would be quick to switch to another product Y or Z if the price of X increases a small amount. X, Y, and Z would constitute a market if consumers would stick with them even if the price for all of them increased a bit. The hypothetical monopolist, then, would raise the price on X, Y, and Z above marginal cost because it would gain profits; the revenues from the markup would exceed lost revenues from fewer sales. The technical test is whether a "small but significant and nontransitory increase in price" (SSNIP) would result in a large enough loss of sales that a hypothetical monopolist would refrain from the price increase. Transferred to the labor context, the question is whether, for a proposed job type, a hypothetical monopsonist could profitably implement a "small but significant and nontransitory reduction in wages," which can be called the SSNRW test. If many accountants would quit from a firm that reduced their wages by a small amount, that firm does not monopsonize the accountant labor market. To determine whether there are separate labor markets for "junior accountant" and "senior accountant," one would determine whether accountants were indifferent between these positions. To take a more intuitive example, law firms often make a distinction between "paralegal" and "legal assistant" positions. Nominally the positions are different, but in practice workers may be indifferent between the two, and firms may look for the same sorts of people to fill both of them, paying them roughly the same. If so, there is one labor market rather than two.

What counts as an SSNRW, and how is it determined? In analysis of product markets, a rule of thumb is 5% for one year. A similar threshold could be used for labor market analysis as well. If a hypothetical monopsonist who employed accountants could reduce wages from (say) $80,000 per year to $76,000 per year, then accountants would compose a labor market. If such a reduction would result in so many quits that the hypothetical monopsonist would lose profits, then it is not really a monopsonist (not even hypothetically), and the labor market should be defined more broadly.

A labor market comprises firms that compete by offering a particular type of job to attract workers with a particular skill set. If only a single firm offers that job or desires that sort of worker and lowers the wage from the competitive amount, many of the workers would accept the lower wage because the alternative would be to undergo retraining or accept a job at another firm that does not exploit the worker's education, skills, or experience.

In some cases, markets may be quite narrow. Labor markets are matching markets, so not only the needs of firms but also the preferences of workers help determine the bounds of the market. Imagine that some paralegals are older and have families and are willing to work only nine to five, while others will stay up all night and work on weekends as the employer requires.[15] If some employers need the second type of paralegal and cannot hire from the first pool, then that second type of paralegal defines a narrower labor market.

One might object that workers are mobile and can easily switch occupations. An accountant may tire of accounting and apply for a job as a manager of a business or go to medical school and start over as a doctor. However, the key question is: When faced with lower wages, how likely is a worker to apply to a different job or to quit a current job? The evidence shows that workers are not very sensitive to wages when choosing where to apply[16] or whether to quit a current job.[17] This limited sensitivity of workers to wages implies that employers have the latitude to lower wages below workers' marginal productivity without causing a large number of workers to quit.

Even though many occupations seem quite similar, the costs of switching occupations is high. Workers are more likely to switch between occupations that are similar in the kinds of tasks that are performed. However, the dissimilarity between tasks performed in different jobs is not the main barrier to transition across occupations;[18] this task dissimilarity accounts for only 14% of the cost of switching occupations.[19] Even between two very similar occupations, moves are hampered by other types of entry costs, including retraining and occupational licensing. Removing all barriers to mobility would increase occupational switches by about 10 times.[20] The upshot is that two occupations that may seem very similar to an outsider may not in fact be substitutes for each other; the cost of switching is high rather than low.

Because of high occupational switching costs, workers do not react sensitively to changes in wages across occupations. The costs of switching across occupations can be estimated by comparing actual occupational switches with the occupational switches that would happen if workers simply went to the highest paying occupation. Using this reasoning, studies estimate that switching occupations can entail a loss between half a year and three years of earnings.[21] These losses are significant, and therefore it is plausible that an employer that monopsonizes an occupation can impose a substantial wage cut without driving away many workers.

Geographic scope. The geographic scope of a labor market is the area where most workers work and live. The academic literature mostly uses the commuting zone (CZ) to define geographic scope. CZs were developed by the U.S. Department of Agriculture,[22] based on patterns of commuting. They are fairly large, often comprising a county or more than one county. CZs are only approximations because some workers may commute across CZs, while others may refuse to take a job at the far end of the CZ in which he or she currently works. A very few labor markets—like the market for CEOs—may be national or international in scope.

The results of the studies analyzing the impact of labor market concentration on wages are robust to different definitions of the geographic scope of the labor market, which suggests that the precise definition does not matter.[23] In a legal analysis, the geographic scope would be determined on a case-by-case basis by how far and by what means of transit workers are willing to commute to a job. If two identical jobs are located in the same city, but because of the pattern of bus and subway lines tend to be held by people who live in different neighborhoods, then those jobs may not be in the same geographic area and hence labor market. The following factors, among many others, may be relevant:

- Some areas have excellent public transportation and uncongested highways. All else equal, the geographic scope of labor markets is greater in these areas than in areas with poor commuting options.
- Some jobs require workers to live nearby because they are on call—specialized medical personnel, for example. The geographic scope will be relatively small.
- Workers will likely commute farther for high-paying jobs than for low-paying jobs. If so, the labor markets for high-paying jobs will have larger geographic scope. And it turns out that workers'

willingness to commute varies across job types even aside from differences in pay.[24]

- Younger workers may be willing to commute farther compared to older married workers or those with children. Jobs held by younger people may have larger labor market areas than jobs held by older people.
- If technological advances enable people to work productively from home—as experience during the COVID-19 pandemic has suggested—then the geographic scope of labor markets may expand dramatically. An accountant may be able to work anywhere in the country or the world, with differences in time zones, the need to coordinate with other workers, and language differences being the relevant factors for determining the geographic scope of the labor market.

Plaintiffs can establish the geographic scope of the labor market by relying on surveys or data that reveal commuting patterns.[25] Once the job type is determined, this type of analysis can determine how far people who currently hold those jobs commute to the defendant and competing employers.

4.3. Labor Markets: Monopsony, Concentration, and Elasticity

Once a labor market is defined, the question for antitrust law is whether one or more firms "dominate" that market. From the standpoint of public policy, the concern is that a firm can pay workers below their marginal revenue product. As we have seen, that can occur for three major reasons: search costs, job differentiation, and concentration. Antitrust law focuses on concentration, although the other factors may play a role in certain cases. A labor market is monopsonistic to the extent that any of these factors enable firms to pay workers below the competitive rate.

In traditional antitrust analysis, a firm's market power is typically defined in terms of market share. A firm with greater than 50% market share in a product market—for some regulators or courts, the threshold is higher—is presumptively a "monopolist" in the sense of being subject to Section 2. The threshold establishes only a presumption because markets are complicated. A firm with 50% share may have greater market power if its competitors are minnows than if it faces another firm with 30%, 40%, or more.

To capture this idea, the HHI is often used to measure market concentration. HHI equals the sum of the squares of the percent of market shares of the firms that sell into a market, multiplied by 10,000. The highest possible HHI is 10,000, which occurs when a market has a single monopolist (100^2 = 10,000). As the number of firms increases indefinitely, HHI approaches (but never quite reaches) zero. HHI can also be used to represent labor market concentration. In labor markets, HHI equals the sum of the squares of the share of the labor market.

As an example, suppose that four employers sell widgets into a national product market. If each firm has a 1% market share, and 96 other firms also have a 1% market share, then the HHI is 100 ($1^2 + 1^2 + . . .$). Suppose further the four employers equally divide the labor market of workers who specialize in making widgets. This means that the HHI for widget specialists is 2,500 ($4 * 25^2$). Suppose also that these firms employ custodians, but so do many non-widget firms. If, say, 1,000 firms in the town hire custodians, and all have a small fraction of the custodian labor market, the HHI for custodians is close to 10. As the example indicates, a firm can have different HHIs in different markets.

Recall from chapter 1 that the Horizontal Merger Guidelines, issued by the DOJ and the FTC, classify markets as unconcentrated (HHI less than 1,500), moderately concentrated (HHI between 1,500 and 2,500), and highly concentrated (HHI above 2,500).[26] These classifications serve as triggers: the government will (generally speaking) allow mergers in unconcentrated product markets and scrutinize those in highly concentrated markets, while taking a moderate approach to those in the middle. Because of the symmetrical nature of labor and product markets, the government (and the law generally) should take the same approach when analyzing labor markets.

Market share or HHI share does not translate into monopoly or market power if the firm or firms cannot actually raise prices over the competitive price—as could be the case if entry barriers are low. However, elasticities and HHI for labor markets are correlated. Across all labor markets, a 10% increase in HHI is associated with a 2.2%

decrease in a measure of the labor supply elasticity.[27] Across markets, wages decline with HHI, even after one controls for the labor supply elasticity; this shows that concentration is an important determinant of wages.[28]

The most direct measure of labor market monopsony is labor supply elasticity. Elasticity of infinity means that a worker will quit (or not take a job) if the wage is reduced even a tiny amount below the competitive wage, while elasticity of zero means that a worker will stay put (or still take a job) even if the wage is reduced significantly. Borrowing from antitrust law, a reasonable starting point is that a monopsony exists—that is, a problem that deserves legal attention of some sort—if an SSNRW (5% is the rule of thumb) will not result in a substantial reduction in employment, given quitting and hiring rates.[29] As a rough point of reference, consider an elasticity of 2, which is common across labor markets.[30] An elasticity of 2 means that a 10% increase in wages entails a 20% increase in a firm's employment. If the elasticity is below 2, then an employer that monopsonizes a labor market can profitably reduce wages by 5%.

Low elasticities are a matter of concern for public policy, but not necessarily for antitrust law, a theme I will return to in chapter 7. To see why, imagine that a firm has 80% of the relevant labor market and underpays its workers. Imagine further that (to take an extreme example) search costs are infinite. (The firm is a secret spy agency that recruits workers by tapping them on the shoulder but is otherwise unknown to people.) If the firm were broken up into two firms with 40% of the labor market, each of the two firms would be able to pay the same below-market wage as the single firm did. Because workers are unable to search, the existence of an additional possible employer does not raise their bargaining power or affect their wages. If the breakup of the original firm does not affect search costs—and there is no reason to think that it would—then it does not affect wages or employment.

Still, either elasticities or a concentration measure like HHI or market share can be used to establish that a firm has market power. Because even a small firm can have market power if search and related frictions exist, a small firm could be sued under Section 2 if it engages in actions to extend its monopoly power into other markets.

4.4. Anticompetitive Acts

In product market cases, plaintiffs can obtain relief under Section 2 only by proving that the defendant monopolist engaged in anticompetitive acts that maintained or extended the monopoly. Many different types of conduct qualify as anticompetitive acts. Because of the lack of successful Section 2 labor market cases, the discussion that follows will unavoidably be speculative. To motivate intuitions, I draw labor market analogies from various well-recognized anticompetitive actions that have been identified as such in product market cases.

Predatory pricing/predatory hiring. A seller with market power may find it profitable to charge customers below-market prices to bankrupt an entrant into a market, then charge above-market prices after that firm disappears. In a typical pattern, a monopolist charges high prices until the entrant materializes, then charges below-market prices to prevent the entrant from acquiring customers, doing so long enough to force the entrant to quit the market, and then raising prices again. While predatory pricing can be difficult to prove, it constitutes illegal anticompetitive behavior.[31]

If predatory pricing is a rational strategy of a monopolist, then "predatory hiring" (or perhaps "predatory waging") is a rational strategy of a labor monopsonist. Imagine that a large employer—say, a hospital—in a small town pays nurses a below-market wage. A new firm enters the market, hoping to attract nurses by charging them a market wage. The incumbent responds by raising wages above the workers' marginal revenue product, drawing on its earlier monopsony profits to fund the temporarily loss-producing strategy. The new firm quits the market because it cannot hire nurses at the market wage; then the incumbent lowers wages or worsens working conditions. The incumbent's behavior would constitute predatory hiring and should be considered unlawful for the same reasons that predatory pricing is.

Refusal to deal. A monopolist can (in theory) violate Section 2 by refusing to deal with a rival, driving it out of business. In the classic example, one of two ski resorts terminated an agreement in which the two resorts made their slopes available to the customers of the other. The Supreme Court held that this behavior could run afoul of Section

2 if there was no legitimate business justification.[32] While subsequent cases narrowed the rule, it has not yet been extinguished.

One can easily imagine similar actions on the labor side. If the two ski resorts drew from a single labor market consisting of (say) ski instructors, and the defendant's refusal to deal drove its rival out of business, then the defendant's power over the labor market as well as the product market would have increased. Indeed, the labor market harm would likely have been worse. The risk that customers would find other ski resorts in other parts of the state or country would have disciplined the remaining ski resort, while the local ski bums are unlikely to move away.

Outsourcing. In recent decades, firms have subcontracted out certain labor functions to other companies. One of countless examples, recounted in an article that appeared in *Politico*, described a medical transcriptionist named Diana Borland who worked for the University of Pittsburgh Medical Center. One day she and her coworkers were called to a meeting:

> The news she heard came as a shock: A UPMC representative stood in front of the group and told them their jobs were being outsourced to a contractor in Massachusetts. The representative told them it wouldn't be a big change, since the contractor, Nuance Communications, would rehire them all for the exact same position and the same hourly pay. There would just be a different name on their paychecks.[33]

Borland's hourly wage was later replaced by a piecework system, and her take-home pay plunged. She later quit.

Outsourcing of this type can be justified. UPMC might have thought that it would do best if it specialized in managing healthcare workers while administrative or logistical workers were supervised by another company. There is nothing inherently wrong with companies focusing on their "core" competencies. Thus, while a traditional manufacturing company would employ line workers, engineers, designers, computer programmers, secretaries, janitors, cafeteria workers, security guards, chauffeurs, event planners, and countless other types of workers, a modern manufacturer like Apple might employ only designers and software programmers, contracting out virtually all the other functions, even manufacturing!

David Weil, who has done much to call attention to the "fissuring" of the workplace, has identified numerous pathologies that accompany outsourcing.[34] What, then, is wrong with it? Weil argues that the dominant firm may outsource to firms that are less likely to obey workplace safety laws, perhaps because they are too small to appear on the radar screens of regulators or are too poor to pay fines or damages. But quite a few outsourcing companies are enormous.

Another possibility is that the business plan of the outsourcing firms is labor monopsony. If hospitals compete with each other for transcriptionists, their wages will be bid up. If the hospitals subcontract to a single employer, that employer can pay monopsony wages. While it may not be in the hospitals' joint interest to contract out to a single company that becomes a monopolist of transcription services as well as a monopsonist of transcriptionists, the hospitals may be unable to resist the short-term incentives that the subcontractor offers them (and would likely be unable to collude to resist them collectively). Or the monopsonist could offer a share of the rents to hospitals in return for its monopsony.

This type of anticompetitive behavior has not been documented, but it seems plausible. While it would violate the antitrust laws, the difficulties of constructing a class of workers and offering proof would be substantial.

Controlling employees. A related idea is that employers create entry barriers to labor markets by preventing or discouraging employees from quitting and going to work for competing employers. Noncompetes—the topic of chapter 6—directly serve this function, but more subtle methods are available as well. Employers can locate the worksite at a distance from the worksites of competitors so that switching jobs would raise commuting costs. They can instill solidarity among their employees with retreats, games, and related activities so that workers will be reluctant to leave the workforce. They can similarly encourage workers to think of competitors as enemies so that the incumbent workers will not consider joining them. Loyalty-enhancing activities of this sort are a species of job differentiation and enhance an employer's power over a worker.

Proving that such activities violate antitrust law would be a challenge. Employers can always argue that they engage in these activities to enhance morale, which increases productivity, and that job differentiation caters to workers' preferences. But these defenses will not always be persuasive. In product market cases, plaintiffs have prevailed with similar arguments. In the Microsoft antitrust case, for example, a court held that Microsoft illegally maintained and extended its monopoly over operating systems by designing Windows so that consumers would be more likely to use Microsoft's browser than competitors' browsers.[35] The court rejected Microsoft's arguments that its design choices improved the consumer's experience. An employer's workplace "design" can be likened to Microsoft's design of its operating system. Where design elements reduce competition without having a legitimate business justification, they are illegal.

4.5. Reform

Section 2 needs to be reformed. The problem is not the statutory language but the lack of cases that provide guidance for workers who are the victims of anticompetitive behavior by monopsonists. To remedy this problem, regulators in the DOJ and the FTC should publish detailed guidance. Failing that, Congress should pass a more detailed version of Section 2 as applied to labor monopsonists.[36] The law should include the following reforms.

Labor market definition. Courts need to understand that labor markets are often narrow—much narrower than product markets. Because of the cost of commuting, a labor market area might be limited to a town, or even a neighborhood or the city center. Labor market areas could have strange shapes because workers will commute only to locations near subway and bus lines. Similarly, the relevant occupation can be narrower than standard definitions found in government documents. Senior workers do not apply for entry-level positions, and beginners do not apply for senior positions—even though the position might have the same title, such as "accountant" or "carpenter." The relevant market can be further limited by the nature of the work—its intensity, flexibility, and so on.

Labor market power. Plaintiffs satisfy the market power requirement that is typically imposed in Section 2 cases by proving that the employer has a "large" share of the labor market. How large is "large"? On the product market side, courts nearly always accept 90%, usually accept above 70%, and occasionally accept shares around 50% or higher.[37] Because of the frictions in labor markets, the 50% figure or an even lower figure seems appropriate for labor-side antitrust litigation under Section 2. Plaintiffs could satisfy these requirements in either of two ways: based on the employer's percentage of employment or based on the employer's percentage of job postings.

Anticompetitive behavior. Plaintiffs would be able to base their case on any of the following anticompetitive acts: mergers in highly concentrated markets; use of noncompete and related clauses; restrictions on employees' freedom to disclose wage and benefit information; unfair labor practices under the National Labor Relations Act;[38] misclassification of employees as independent contractors; no-poaching, wage-fixing, and related agreements that are also presumptively illegal under Section 1; and prohibitions on class actions. Of course, current law gives employees the theoretical right to allege these types of anticompetitive behavior, but the cases show a pattern of judicial skepticism, as noted earlier. Codification would help employees by compelling courts to take these claims seriously. Employers would be allowed to rebut a prima facie case of anticompetitive behavior by showing that the act in question would likely lead to an increase in wages.

This reform would strengthen and extend Section 2 actions against labor monopsonists by standardizing a list of anticompetitive acts. While not all of these acts are invariably anticompetitive, the employer would be able to defend itself by citing a business justification. For example, a noncompete could be justified because it protects an employer's investment in training. If so, an employer could avoid antitrust liability by showing that its use of noncompetes benefits workers, who obtain higher wages as a result of their training.[39]

These reforms would strengthen Section 2 claims against labor monopsonies but would also preserve the doctrinal structure of Section 2. They would not generate significant legal uncertainty or require a revision in the way that we think about antitrust law.

5

Mergers

MERGER REVIEW IS ONE of the most important antitrust functions of the FTC and the DOJ. When large firms agree to merge, they are required by law to inform these agencies ahead of the merger. The agencies then review the merger proposal and either block it or allow the merger to proceed. If the agencies block the merger, the firms will either abandon the merger or litigate it. Section 7 of the Clayton Act prohibits mergers, acquisitions, and related transactions if "the effect of such acquisition may be substantially to lessen competition, or to tend to create a monopoly."[1] Antitrust agencies and courts interpret this language to mean that if a merger results in substantial concentration of the market, the merger is illegal, unless the merging parties can prove that despite the increased concentration, prices will decline—presumably as a result of greater economies of scale or other cost savings. Notably, the merger standards, which are embodied in the Horizontal Merger Guidelines, say nothing about *wages*. And, indeed, the FTC and DOJ have never blocked a merger based on labor market effects. This is a serious mistake, for which there is no justification. There is substantial evidence that mergers can increase labor market concentration and reduce wages as a result.[2] Fortunately, in the past few years, as the problem of labor market concentration began to attract attention, agency officials have begun to incorporate labor market analysis into merger review.

When competitors merge, the merger is called "horizontal." When firms at different levels of a supply chain merge, the merger is "vertical." Horizontal mergers are more dangerous than vertical mergers because they directly reduce competition. The possible anticompetitive effects of vertical mergers are more subtle, and in recent years courts have reacted with skepticism to arguments that vertical mergers should be enjoined. For that reason, this chapter focuses on horizontal mergers.

Many mergers or acquisitions occur under the radar of the antitrust agencies because the notification threshold is not met. Some commentators believe that private equity firms have attempted to obtain market power in both product and labor markets by buying up independent practices of various types—dentists' offices, medical clinics, nail salons, physical therapy practices—and linking them into chains that dominate a local product or labor market.[3] Affected customers and workers can sue under the antitrust laws, but this type of litigation can be challenging. A journalistic account suggests that the merger of large farm equipment firms—approved by the government presumably because the firms competed in a national or international product market—led to mergers of farm equipment dealers in rural areas, which in turn reduced employment opportunities for farm equipment repair workers. The dealer mergers would not have met the notification threshold but nonetheless reduced competition in the labor market, resulting in suppressed wages and lower employment.[4]

5.1. Market Concentration

The risk posed by a merger is that it increases market concentration, which can cause harm in two different ways. In product markets, a firm that gains market power through concentration can raise prices by reducing output ("unilateral effects").[5] And as the number of firms declines, the remaining firms can more easily engage in either explicit or implicit collusion, such as parallel pricing, which also results in higher prices and reduced output ("coordinated effects").[6] Mergers pose the same risks to labor markets. A firm that gains power in the labor market may be able to reduce wages and employment; when the number of employers declines, the remaining employers can more easily engage in implicit or explicit collusion with the same effects.

The Horizontal Merger Guidelines hence treat increases in market concentration as a trigger for scrutiny. The Guidelines divide markets into unconcentrated (HHI less than 1,500), moderately concentrated

(HHI between 1,500 and 2,500), and highly concentrated (HHI above 2,500). If the post-merger product market remains unconcentrated, or the merger increases the HHI by fewer than 100 points, the government generally allows the merger. If the merger results in a moderately concentrated market and an increase of the HHI by more than 100 points, then the government will scrutinize the merger. If the merger results in a highly concentrated market along with an HHI increase of 100 to 200 points, the merger will also receive scrutiny, and if the HHI increase exceeds 200 points, the merger is subject to a rebuttable presumption that it is illegal, as I discuss below.

Because of the symmetry of product market and labor market concentration, the government should use the same standard to evaluate the effects of mergers on labor markets. It is of course possible that the relationship between labor-market HHI and wage suppression is different from the relationship between product-market HHI and price markups, but until further research clarifies the difference between these relationships, the existing Guidelines provide a sensible starting point.

The market definition and concentration (MDC) approach to merger analysis can be used to analyze the labor market effects of mergers just as it is used to analyze the product market effects of mergers. Imagine, for example, that two nationwide firms announce a plan to merge— say, the two food-processing companies Tyson and Perdue. While the companies sell processed chicken and other food products into national (or international) markets, they rely on local labor markets. The regulator would be required to examine the markets one by one. In many geographic areas, there may be one or more facilities owned only by one of the two merging companies. In those places, the merger does not increase labor market concentration. In other areas, both firms may own facilities, and in those areas, the merger will likely increase concentration for one or more occupations. The regulator would need to look at each job type (including, for example, the people who eviscerate chickens, the IT folk, the accountants, the administrators) and determine the impact of the merger on that specific labor market. Most likely (though not necessarily), a merger between two food processors will have an impact on labor markets that employ food-processing specialists but not more general labor markets like IT technicians. Where the HHI increases substantially, a remedy will be necessary: either the spinning-off of facilities to other companies or injunction of the merger.

While the analysis may seem elaborate, it is not more complicated than many product-market merger analyses. While a merger between Tyson and Perdue would mostly affect national product markets, and so may seem simpler, many mergers affect numerous local product markets. For example, when drug store chains merge, the regulators must examine every local product market—every area in the country where, before the merger, people can choose to patronize stores owned by both chains. However, because labor markets are almost always local, while product markets are frequently national, review of mergers for their labor market effects will add substantial work to the merger review process.

Some commentators believe that the MDC approach does not make sense even for product markets, and therefore should not be used for labor markets as well.[7] The MDC approach can be derived from standard economic models of oligopoly, which show that firms gain less by raising prices over marginal cost as their market share declines. But the derivation depends on strong assumptions that may not be sufficiently realistic to justify heavy reliance on MDC. Some readers might wonder where the various HHI thresholds come from, and the answer is that they are, to some extent, arbitrary. My purpose here is not to defend the MDC approach but to argue that if the MDC approach is accepted for product markets (as it is by the government and courts), then it should be used for labor markets as well. Otherwise, firms that are thwarted in their efforts to raise prices by merging with product market rivals will naturally be led to merge with labor market rivals to lower the cost of labor.

5.2. Downward Wage Pressure

In recent years, the MDC approach in product markets has lost ground to the upward pricing pressure (UPP) approach. The UPP is more closely tied to credible economic models of unilateral effects than the MDC approach is. Because UPP was invented recently,[8] it has not played as important a role in litigation as MDC has, but it does receive a brief mention, and the government's imprimatur, in the Merger

Guidelines.[9] Like MDC, UPP has been used only to analyze the product market effects of mergers. But the analogous idea of downward wage pressure (DWP) for labor market harms could be used. DWP uses two key terms: "markdown" and "diversion ratio." These two terms correspond roughly to market concentration and the increase in concentration caused by the merger, as they measure the degree of preexisting market power and the increased market power created by the merger.

Markdown. To measure preexisting market power rather than define a market and measure its concentration, UPP more directly measures the extent to which firms, prior to the merger, can hold wages below their competitive level. This is measured by the "markup," the percent by which the price the firm's charge exceeds the marginal cost that it would charge under competition.

In labor markets, we instead consider the mark*down.* The markdown is the percent by which the wage falls below the worker's marginal revenue product. (To be precise, the markdown equals 100 times the ratio of the gap between the marginal revenue product and the wage.) The markdown for each merging firm may be different. And markdowns can be measured by using either accounting data from firms or econometric studies that measure the elasticity of residual labor supply.

Diversion ratio. To measure the degree to which a merger will tend to increase market power, the UPP approach uses the concept of a "diversion ratio" rather than the increase in concentration caused by a merger. Consider, for example, the calculations that would go into a merger of GM and Ford. Before the merger, GM earns a profit on each car equal to revenue minus marginal costs. When it decides whether to sell an additional car by lowering its price, it makes a trade-off: it sells more cars (while Ford sells fewer cars), but it earns less profit (or "markup") per car as its price falls. The optimal price balances these two forces.

Now imagine that the two automakers merge. To understand the effect of the merger on the firm's pricing decision, one can usefully imagine that GM and Ford continue as divisions of the merged entity. The CEO of the merged entity directs the division head of GM and the division head of Ford to maximize profits for the merged entity, not for the individual divisions. The GM head will think as follows. When GM lowers its price to sell a car, the merged entity not only forgoes the higher markups per GM car that comes with a higher price. The merged entity also loses the markups on Ford cars that are not sold because of the additional sales of GM cars at the lower price. The opportunity cost of the lost sale of a Ford car enters GM's calculations, resulting in a weaker incentive for the GM division head to lower prices (or a stronger incentive to increase prices). The same is true for the Ford division head.

These effects can be represented as *diversion ratios*. The GM-to-Ford diversion ratio is the fraction of additional Ford sales that are diverted from GM (rather than from another car company or that are new sales that would not otherwise have been made) when Ford lowers its prices. A diversion ratio is calculated from Ford to GM as well.

In the case of labor market effects, an analogous analysis is performed. When two food processors seek to merge, the analyst calculates diversion ratios with respect to their workers. The diversion ratio for each merging firm is the fraction of workers who would quit and join the other merging firm (rather than joining a nonmerging firm or dropping out of the labor market) if the first firm lowers wages.

The diversion ratio measures the extent to which a merger increases market power more directly than HHI does. Market definitions are crude and mask heterogeneity among workers and their relationships with employers. Diversion ratios can capture this complexity. Another advantage of diversion ratios is that they are easier to estimate than market definitions are. One natural proxy for diversion ratios is turnover. Surveys and other methods can determine the fraction of workers at Firm 1 who move to Firm 2 rather than to other firms or out of the labor market. If Firm 1 and Firm 2 then merge, this ratio provides a starting point for estimating the diversion ratio. Another source of information that can be used to estimate the diversion ratio is job hunting data. This data source reveals information about where workers interview; if many of Firm 1's hires also interviewed at Firm 2, this suggests that the two firms compete for workers, and hence that a merger between them will reduce labor market competition.

Effects. The DWP index for Employer A is the markdown *of Employer B* multiplied by the diversion ratio *from Employer B to Employer A*. To understand why, consider the difference between what happens to Employer A's finances if it lowers wages pre-merger and if it lowers wages post-merger. To hire an additional worker pre-merger, Employer

A must raise its wage. The worker it hires will, with a chance equal to the diversion ratio, be taken from Employer B, but Employer A really does not care where the worker comes from.

After the merger, this changes. Employer A now cares about the profits earned by Employer B. If the worker is diverted from Employer B, Employer A now effectively suffers a loss equal to the markdown Employer B was earning off that employee. This loss occurs with a probability equal to the diversion ratio from Employer B to Employer A, and thus the product of the B-to-A diversion ratio with B's markdown constitutes the additional cost of an additional employee A faces after the merger that it did not face before the merger.

The DWP does not directly tell us how much the worker's wages will fall. Instead, it tells us the *tax* on wages to which the merger is equivalent. The merger taxes wages because it makes hiring the worker effectively more expensive for the employers. How much of this tax is passed through to workers as a decreased wage and how much will be absorbed by the employer and/or passed through to consumers as higher prices depends on market conditions, usually summarized as the "pass-through rate."[10] In some cases worker wages may fall by even more than the amount of this tax.

UPP numbers are usually compared to some small standard threshold, like 1%–2%, to determine whether cases are worth reviewing. A 1%–2% tax on wages is a material weight on the decision of firms. Of course, any positive DWP is a cause for concern, but authorities have typically assumed in product markets that there are some efficiency gains from mergers, perhaps on the order of 1%–2%, that are likely to offset at least some harms from reduced competition. Analogously it seems reasonable as a starting point to flag for serious consideration mergers where DWP for both firms exceeds 2% and to give less scrutiny to mergers where both are below 1%. Intermediate cases must be carefully considered.

Comments. The DWP, like the MDC, should be understood as a relatively simple proxy that provides guidance to regulated parties but only an approximation of the underlying social value of a proposed merger. It is not clear whether the MDC or the DWP is a better rule, or in fact whether either of them is always the better approach; they might work better in different market settings. The MDC is better established and draws on long experience of the agencies and courts. The DWP seems more theoretically sound, and recent work has continued to refine it as well as provide reason to believe that it may work better than the MDC.

A virtue of both approaches is that they are flexible and can be easily modified if further evidence suggests that they are too strict or not strict enough. In the case of the MDC, one can raise or lower the HHI thresholds to make merger challenges harder or easier. In the case of the DWP, one can adjust the assumed efficiency level of a merger.

A last point concerns the complexity of many mergers, which can have different effects in different markets. A merger can reduce competition in both product markets and labor markets, and it can reduce competition in some geographic (product) markets and not others, and the same with labor markets. Consider, for example, the merger of two nationwide hospital chains. The merger might reduce the number of rival hospitals in big city X from 15 to 14 and the number of rival hospitals in small town Y from 3 to 2. Obviously, the product market and labor market effects will be greater in the small town than in the big city. But even within the small town, the product market and labor market effects are likely to be different. If there is no other place to obtain medical care, the product market effects will be significant. However, if the small town happens to have a large retirement community with assisted-living facilities, where nurses are frequently employed, then it is possible that the labor market effects of the merger—with respect to the market in nurses—is less severe. Most employers offer multiple jobs, just as most producers offer many products, and the rich interactions between the many products or jobs of one merging firm with the many products or jobs of the other must be considered. When evaluating mergers, all these complex product and labor market effects must be considered, and remedies (as in the case of traditional merger analysis) might involve spinning off some of the underlying entities in some of the markets.

5.3. Other Factors in Merger Analysis

The mathematical analysis of mergers is accompanied by informal analysis that looks at factors the existing models exclude. These factors include efficiency gains of mergers, entry into the market, and external influences on firm conduct. Informal analysis is even more important for labor markets than for product markets because formal models of many important features of labor markets for merger analysis have not yet been developed.

Efficiencies. The most important factors considered at this stage of merger analysis are "efficiencies" that may make the merger socially beneficial despite its anticompetitive effects. Such efficiencies fall into three categories: productive efficiencies associated with economies of scale or network effects; contracting efficiencies and other ways in which the merger may reduce market power or facilitate commerce; and what might be called "viability efficiencies," referring to the possibility that one merging party might exit the market or become unviable as a competitor in the absence of the merger, in which case the merger merely hastens that party's exit from the scene.[11] While these efficiencies are sometimes quantifiable, they are typically addressed in qualitative fashion.

Just as product cost may fall with an efficiency-enhancing merger, labor productivity could increase. For example, a single large factory might be able to produce airplanes more efficiently than two small factories because the large factory can subdivide the assembly line to achieve greater gains from labor specialization. The increase in labor market productivity may cause labor demand to increase or decrease, depending on the structure of the product market.

Under the Merger Guidelines, the merging firms are permitted to argue that the efficiencies justify a merger that otherwise would be deemed anticompetitive.[12] However, this type of defense is subject to two important limits. First, the "consumer welfare" standard implies that the efficiency gain must be large enough so consumers benefit despite an increase in market power—that the firm's costs decline enough that even with additional market power, the firm will charge prices below those that prevailed before the merger.[13] In contrast, if consumers pay higher prices, the efficiency does not count in favor of the merger even if the firm's profits are greater than the consumers' loss.[14]

Second, the relevant efficiencies must be *merger-specific* in the sense that they are possible, or possible at reasonable cost, only through the merger.[15] For example, if two wireless carriers could and naturally would (but for the prospect of a merger) interconnect their networks so that subscribers to both carriers could benefit from the network of the other, these carriers could not use the prospect of shared networks as a merger defense. If the carriers can connect their networks at reasonable cost through contract, they cannot claim that a merger is necessary.

These principles carry over naturally, in suitably modified form, to the analysis of merger effects on labor markets, though a few subtle issues arise. Many of the same factors that could act as efficiencies on the product side are also efficiencies on the labor side. By analogy to the "consumer welfare" standard, mergers that trigger scrutiny by reducing labor market competition should be subject to a "worker welfare" standard.[16] The fact that the merger might raise firm profits more than it harms workers should not be sufficient to excuse the merger. Instead, the merger would be permitted if it sufficiently increases worker productivity (workers' marginal revenue product) in a way that will not fully be absorbed by lower prices or increased employer profits. Thus, harms from reduced competition are more than fully offset, and therefore workers' wages, benefits, or conditions will improve because of the merger.

This is not to say that mergers that harm workers should never be approved. The losses to workers could be offset by gains elsewhere in the economy. Indeed, the merger of two firms that operate in a frictionless labor market should not greatly harm workers even if it does result in significant layoffs, because in a competitive labor market the laid-off workers can easily find equally good jobs.[17] In contrast, a merger that *does* create competitive concern should not be excused simply on the basis that it allows the firm to cut costs by destroying jobs. Antitrust law does not allow such a trade-off, nor should it.[18]

In some cases, a merger may prove overall competitively harmful in labor markets (viz. harm worker welfare) and beneficial in product markets (viz. benefit consumer welfare). Such cases should be treated roughly like ones where competitive harm occurs in one product market but there are competitive benefits in another product market. To the extent possible, antitrust authorities should try to find remedies that address the competitive harms while preserving the benefits, such as requiring the spinning-off of units that would allow an increase in market power. However, the frequency of such cases should not be exaggerated; mergers that increase labor market power and thus raise effective costs will not usually bring lower prices to consumers, and mergers increasing product market power and thus reducing sales will not typically create great jobs. As I emphasized earlier, enforcers should not be fooled by the fallacy that after "decreasing labor costs" using monopsony, an employer would pass such gains through to consumers. Monopsony power raises the effective marginal cost a firm faces and thus should almost always lead to increased prices.

The broad category of efficiencies considered in mergers relate to the so-called double marginalization problem and other complementarities in the production or consumption of the products of the merging firms. Firms that supply complementary products to a consumer or that supply intermediate inputs to each other may, absent a merger, each demand a markup on their own product, leading to the stacking of markups in a manner that reduces both firm profits and consumer welfare.[19] A recent example involves the providers of premium cable channels, often regional sports networks, which have sometimes merged with cable companies. Research has found that such mergers generally lead to lower marginal channel prices for consumers purchasing from the merging cable company because the internalization of the channel provider's profits by the cable company induces lower prices (though such mergers may also have anticompetitive foreclosure effects).[20]

Such mergers are said to have a "vertical component" as well as the "horizontal component" that causes antitrust concern. For example, a household paper goods firm mostly complements a grocery store that sells a high volume of its products but may also compete with a house brand of the grocery store. A merger may thus have both vertical benefits and horizontal harms that must be balanced to determine the net competitive effect. Matters are similar in labor markets. Jobs may be complementary to each other directly because workers are complementary. For example, the researchers at a company that mostly invents new products may be more productive if they merge with another company that is focused on commercialization of new products. The two groups of workers may be able to interact with each other and cooperate more closely if they work for the same firm than if they work for different firms, even if those firms cooperate via contract.

The final viability efficiency consideration that arises in many mergers is the possibility that, but for the merger, one of the merger partners would go out of business or otherwise would become an ineffectual competitor in the market. This issue often arises for firms that are either near bankruptcy or that are losing money in some critical markets. To the extent that it can be demonstrated that absent the merger the firm would exit and that the competitive harm of the merger is less than that of exit by the failing firm (or that the merger could strengthen the competitive position of the nonfailing merger partner), the merger will typically be allowed to proceed. In labor markets similar arguments may be relevant: that an employer would otherwise "ship the factory to China" may be used to defend a merger. However, as in product markets, it will usually be necessary to demonstrate that there was no other feasible route to stabilize the profitability of the business, such as selling it to an alternative purchaser who is not a direct competitor.

Entry and potential competition. Mergers (and especially anticompetitive mergers) tend to encourage firm entry. To the extent that the merging firms raise prices and compete less intensely, they leave profit opportunities for a new firm to exploit. In principle, this tendency to encourage entry may be a reason for excusing the anticompetitive effects of entry. Some commentators, however, are skeptical that firms can enter markets as easily as this theory suggests.

Whoever is right, this argument is even weaker for labor markets. Extensive labor market frictions deter entry. In the product market case, a firm can enter a market merely by supplying products identical to or like those being sold by the merged firm. In the labor market case, a firm can in principle enter a market by hiring workers laid off by merging firms, but the new entrant will need to duplicate hard-to-observe workplace conditions that may have attracted the workers originally, and also contend with a workforce that was demoralized by the earlier layoffs. Views within the economics community have drifted in this direction.[21]

Another increasingly important factor in the analysis of mergers in product markets is their effect on *potential* competition. Instagram may not have directly competed with Facebook at the time Facebook purchased Instagram, but Facebook may have been rightly concerned that Instagram might, if left to itself, succeed in reorienting the social media landscape around images rather than the image-text mixture that Facebook had profited from.

Purchases to forestall potential competition may also take place when firms fear competition in the labor market. In recent years, tech companies have rushed to hire programmers who specialize in machine learning. A common way of acquiring such talent is to purchase machine-learning start-ups: Google bought DeepMind, Microsoft bought Maluuba, Apple bought Lattice Data. In contrast, the tech companies could have tried to hire workers directly by luring them from the incumbent employers with promises of high compensation. It seems likely that the share of the gains accruing to workers (as opposed to investors and the few at the top of these start-ups) from open competition would have been greater than under an acquisition strategy. The acquisition thus effectively killed off potential competition for workers. Analyses of potential labor market competition, especially in a highly dynamic labor market, should form a part of antitrust analysis of the labor market harms from mergers. This type of threat may not be easily gauged by the standard MDC and UPP/DWP approaches, which focus on the present state of competition rather than the future competitive landscape.

Vertical mergers. Antitrust law takes a more relaxed attitude toward vertical mergers than horizontal mergers because vertical mergers do not as frequently consolidate product markets. But certain vertical mergers pose risks. Suppose an upstream seller (a manufacturer or other supplier) possesses market power and merges with one of two (or a few) downstream buyers. The merged firm then sells to the other downstream buyer (or buyers) at an elevated price, giving itself (in its capacity as downstream firm, the result of the merger) a competitive advantage. This is known as "foreclosure" and is illegal under the antitrust laws.

Downstream product and labor markets behave similarly in this case. Suppose the market for nursing aides has two hospitals in it, both of which serve patients covered by the same HMO. Now suppose the HMO acquires Hospital 1 and lowers reimbursement rates for patients served at Hospital 2. This will lower labor market demand for nursing aides in Hospital 2 and give Hospital 1 the ability to lower wages for its own nursing aides.

Appendix. Case Study: The Effect of Hospital Mergers on the Labor Market for Nurses

Suppose two hospitals, each with one-third of the nurses in a CZ, propose a merger.[22] Should the government block the merger because of its labor market effects? We can use existing evidence to calculate the predicted fall in nurse wages and check if the two approaches we have discussed generate results consistent with the evidence.

MDC. The merger would increase the HHI from 3,333 to 5,556, for a difference of 2,223.[23] Under the Merger Guidelines, the proposed merger would be presumptively blocked because of the high initial HHI and the high increase in HHI. Barry Hirsch and Edward Schumacher estimate the effect of hospital concentration on nurses' log wages and find (when controlling for fixed effects) that the coefficient on hospital concentration is −0.4, which implies that the merger would lower nurse wages by almost 9%.[24] A more recent study by Azar, Marinescu, and Steinbaum finds a log HHI point estimate of −0.12 (and a mean baseline HHI of 0.3), so the implied increase in HHI would decrease wages by 20%.[25] Thus, given an average annual salary of $68,500 for registered nurses,[26] the merger would lower their salary by $6,165 to $13,700 while also eliminating some jobs. The hospitals could try to rebut by showing that efficiency savings would allow them to raise wages. It is possible, for example, that nursing labor can be used more efficiently in one hospital than in two, but the merging hospitals would need to prove an efficiency gain of sufficient magnitude.

DWP. In a symmetric merger, the UPP reduces to m*D, where D is the diversion ratio and m is the markup. Some algebra reveals that the analogous measure for the labor market case would be the same, m*D, with m now the markdown. Staiger, Spetz, and Phibbs estimate a residual labor supply elasticity facing the hospital of 0.1,[27] which would imply a markdown of 10, and the symmetry of the merger would imply D = 0.5, and so DWP =.5*10 = 5. Hence labor productivity would have to more than double after the merger in order to keep wages constant in this example. Again, the burden would be on the merging hospitals to prove this efficiency gain. While other studies have produced different estimates of residual labor supply elasticity of nurses and other healthcare workers, the better work suggests lower numbers, and so high DWPs.[28] This strongly suggests that many hospital mergers should be carefully watched for labor market effects, in sharp contrast to the status quo.

Defenses. How might hospitals defend a merger that increases labor market power? One possibility, noted above, is that a merger could reduce redundancy. Another possibility would be increased productivity because of greater ease of medical record sharing or cross-hospital referrals. The merging parties would have to show that these were likely to increase wages and could not be achieved without a merger. Other informal factors seem important here, especially changes to hours, benefits, and job descriptions, as these can be highly specific to a particular hospital and nurses can be asked to work odd hours. Cutting in the other direction, barriers to entry are high in the medical care market. Moreover, the prospect of coordinated effects might be important given the close geographic proximity of hospitals and their frequent communication about community health, which may serve as an opportunity for collusion on wages.

6

Noncompetes

FOR MANY YEARS, JIMMY JOHN'S franchises included a covenant not to compete (or "noncompete") in the employment contracts signed by their workers, including entry-level sandwich makers. The noncompete barred employees from working for any sandwich shop within three miles of any Jimmy John's franchise for two years.[1] Because thousands of Jimmy John's outlets are scattered across the United States, most of them concentrated in cities, the noncompete barred sandwich-shop work over huge swaths of the country, including major urban areas. A public outcry and litigation ensued. The noncompetes were likely illegal because they did not protect trade secrets or customer goodwill but may well have deterred low-income workers from seeking higher-paying jobs from Jimmy John's competitors. Jimmy John's eventually settled litigation brought by state attorneys general and withdrew the noncompetes.[2]

Noncompetes are clauses in employment contracts that forbid workers to work for competitors of their former employer for a certain period of time and over a defined geographic area.[3] Despite its traditional orientation toward laissez faire, the common law has always regarded noncompetes as restraints of trade, and hence presumptively unenforceable. Noncompetes are subject to a reasonableness test: a noncompete is enforceable only if the restrictions it imposes on the worker are no more burdensome than necessary to protect the employer's legitimate business interest—usually in protection of trade secrets or customer goodwill. In practice, however, noncompetes are frequently enforced, or simply not challenged. New research by Evan Starr and his coauthors reveals that they appear in millions of employment contracts and may deter workers from quitting and seeking alternative employment.[4] While noncompetes were traditionally understood to be justified only for specialized and well-compensated employees, it turns out they are frequently imposed on low-skill employees like the Jimmy John's sandwich makers.[5]

The common law approach is plainly inadequate because employers do not face substantial sanctions if a court invalidates a noncompete, and—more significant—the common law does not provide the right approach for evaluating noncompetes. Because noncompetes pose a threat to competition, the analytic lens of antitrust law should be used. Antitrust law focuses on the market effects of noncompetes and provides for a significant deterrent in the form of treble damages when employers abuse them. However, antitrust enforcement has rarely been successful because of difficulties of proof. Accordingly, I argue for a stronger antitrust regime that incorporates presumptions derived from the empirical literature on noncompetes and related labor market behavior. The law should treat noncompetes as presumptively illegal, allowing employers to rebut the presumption if they can prove that the noncompetes they use will benefit rather than harm their workers.

6.1. The Law of Noncompetes

Legal regulation of noncompetes goes back centuries. Noncompetes originated in the medieval system of apprenticeship, which was the chief method by which specialized craft skills were transferred across generations.[6] A master craftsman would employ an apprentice, who would be bound to serve for a period of years. The apprentice was usually young; he (always he) would live with the craftsman and engage in (often menial) work and (in theory) receive training. The apprentice was paid little or nothing beyond room and board, but once he completed his apprenticeship, he would be able to offer the services he had learned. Eventually, he, too, would be recognized as a master craftsman, would be able to charge for his work, and would take on apprentices. Guilds would enforce these rules, as would the state through its court system. Eventually, some masters demanded that their apprentices sign a noncompete so as to protect themselves from competition after those apprentices had completed their apprenticeships. In the first reported noncompete opinion in England, *John Dyer's Case*, which was decided in 1414,[7] one of the judges suggested that a noncompete might be illegal because it prevented the former apprentice from practicing the trade for which he was trained. This view reflected a customary norm enforced by guilds[8] and would influence the development of the common law.[9]

The modern common law rule was recognized by the early 18th century, in a case called *Mitchel v. Reynolds*.[10] Although that case involved a noncompete that was ancillary to the sale of a business rather than an employee noncompete, it established the common-law framework that was to be used for both types of noncompetes.

Whenever an employer seeks to enforce a noncompete, the court requires the employer to identify the business interest that the noncompete was designed to protect. The "protectable interest," as it sometimes is called, must usually be either goodwill or trade secrets.[11] In some jurisdictions, courts have also recognized that a protectable interest may encompass investments in training.[12] A common type of case involves goodwill in the form of customer lists that have been entrusted to an employee. A noncompete ensures that an employee will not quit, find work with a competitor, and use the customer list to poach the original employer's customers. To show a protectable interest in a customer list, the employer must show that the customer list was secret, that it was entrusted to the employee, that the employee used it to make sales, and that the employee's involvement in sales was deep and personal enough that the customers might transfer their loyalty from the firm to the employee. The underlying concern is that if an employer has invested in a customer list and cannot protect it from its competitors, the employer may not share the list with employees, or may share it in a restricted way that undermines its business. That is why the employer cannot claim a protectable interest when the list is public or when the employee does not know the customers well enough to persuade them to drop the original employer for a new employer.

The New York Court of Appeals' decision in the frequently cited case of *Reed, Roberts Associates, Inc. v. Strauman*[13] represents typical "protectable interest" analysis of noncompetes under the common law. Strauman was a senior vice president in charge of operations at a firm that advised employers on compliance with state unemployment laws and related laws. He quit and joined a competing firm. The former employer sued to enforce a noncompete. The court ruled against the employer. While Strauman was an important employee with significant oversight duties, he was not privy to trade secrets and he did not memorize or record the employer's customer list. And while he had knowledge of the employer's operations that could potentially be used to improve the operations of the competitor, this knowledge was not a protected interest. By contrast, in *Webcraft Technologies, Inc. v. McCaw*,[14] the court enforced a noncompete where the employer had entrusted the defendant with secret customer lists and trade secrets like the prices charged to various customers. The court pointed out that acquiring a customer was an "arduous" process that took months or years of negotiation. The defendant had copied or memorized the customer list and trade secrets and supplied them to her new employer.

If the employer establishes a protectable interest, it then must show that the noncompete is tailored to that interest. The courts look at three dimensions of tailoring.[15] First, the noncompete may cover only the relevant industry. If the employee sells shoes, then the noncompete may not prohibit the selling of computer hardware. Second, the noncompete cannot extend beyond a reasonable geographic area. If the employer sells shoes only in the town, the noncompete cannot extend to the suburbs or the state—unless the employer can show (for example) that people from outside of town travel to the town to buy those shoes. Third, the noncompete may not extend too long in duration. In the case of customer relationships, for example, the noncompete may give the employer only enough time to hire a replacement and train her to perform the old employee's job in a satisfactory fashion. Then competition must be permitted.[16]

These general rules apply with remarkable consistency across jurisdictions, but there are also many variations. Some courts define protectable interests broadly to encompass any "legitimate economic interest,"[17] while others limit them to trade secrets, confidential information, and some limited forms of goodwill—in Illinois, for example, "relations with near-permanent customers of the employer."[18] Courts disagree about whether an investment in training counts as a protectable interest.[19] Courts also disagree about the appropriate duration and geographic scope of noncompetes and whether noncompetes must be supported by additional consideration. Courts take different remedial approaches as well. Some courts refuse to enforce noncompetes that are overbroad, while others shave off the overbroad portion but enforce the noncompete to the extent justified by the employer's protectable interest.

Unhappy with the weak common-law regime, some employees have challenged noncompetes under the antitrust laws. Noncompetes were and are common-law restraints of trade, and they are clearly covered by the Sherman Act.[20] However, antitrust litigation against noncompetes has been infrequent. As late as 1973, a scholar was unable to find a single case that applied the federal antitrust laws to employee noncompetes.[21] In fact, I was able to find two cases from that era,[22] but while, since then, many more cases have been reported, these cases have been notably unsuccessful. A search in the Westlaw database yielded a grand total of zero cases in which an employee noncompete was successfully challenged under the antitrust laws.[23]

6.2. The Benefits of Noncompetes for Labor Markets

Noncompetes reduce job mobility for workers. Reduction in mobility benefits the employer by enabling it to recover investments in training a worker and to protect certain intangible assets of the firm. These benefits are social benefits as well; they should be distributed to customers as lower prices, investors as higher returns, and workers as higher wages. At the same time, the noncompete reduces the worker's bargaining power by eliminating or weakening the threat to quit in order to obtain a better job. In principle, the worker will demand ex ante compensation in the form of higher wages. But it is unclear that workers do demand such compensation. Moreover, employers probably cannot credibly commit to pay higher compensation in the long term or not to degrade working conditions so as to offset the compensation. More important, noncompetes produce negative externalities: even if the employer adequately compensates the employee, a noncompete can harm competition by preventing other firms from hiring employees whom they need in order to achieve the scale of production necessary to take market share from the incumbent employer. Below, these benefits and cost of noncompetes are described in greater detail.

The cases and academic scholarship recognize that a noncompete can serve a legitimate interest for an employer. Curiously, however, the cases and the scholarship put emphasis on different types of interests. I divide the universe of interests into two: investment theories (that is, investment in human capital) and asset theories (or, more precisely, investment in intangible assets that are complementary to human capital).

Investment theories. The investment theory of the noncompete appears to have originated in an article by Paul Rubin and Peter Shedd, which was published in 1981.[24] Rubin and Shedd took as their starting point Gary Becker's theory of human capital.[25] Becker divided human capital into two types: specific and general. Specific human capital consists of a worker's abilities, where those abilities have productive value only for the firm that employs the worker. General human capital consists of abilities that have productive value in other firms as well. For example, a worker who has been trained in the proprietary accounting software used by her employer to manage its internal accounts has specific human capital, to the extent that this training could not be put to use at another employer. In contrast, a worker who has been trained in accounting software that is used at other employers has general human capital.

Becker argued that firms have an optimal incentive to invest in specific human capital—because they alone would obtain the returns from it—and no incentive to invest in general human capital. A firm will not invest in general human capital because the worker who receives it will either quit and go to work for another firm at a higher wage or will demand a higher wage from the original firm. Becker concluded that workers, rather than firms, will invest in general human capital, borrowing if necessary to finance the training investment.

Becker's theory is inconsistent with the evidence.[26] Firms do invest in the general human capital of their workers. For example, law firms train associates to take depositions, write briefs, and conduct examinations of witnesses—skills that these employees can take to other legal jobs. A notable example comes from Germany, where it is common for workers to serve apprenticeships with employers, who provide them with intensive training in general skills.[27] Upon completion of the training the workers receive certificates from third parties that verify they have obtained the relevant skills. This means that other employers know exactly the type of training that the employees have received and that the training was successful, and so have a strong incentive to lure them away from the original employer with a higher wage. These apprenticeships contradict Becker's theory that firms will not invest in general human capital.

Rubin and Shedd proposed that the noncompete solves the puzzle of investment in general human capital. To ensure that it obtains returns on its investment in human capital, the employer can block the worker from working for an outside employer. This gives the worker the choice between quitting and becoming unemployed (or working outside the scope of the noncompete, normally at a lower wage) or continuing to work with the original employer at the negotiated wage. In effect, the employee funds her training in general skills by borrowing from the employer rather than by borrowing from a bank, and the implicit interest on the loan takes the form of a discount on the wage—a wage less than what the employee could earn from another employer. Rubin and Shedd argue that an employer can serve as a more effective financer than a bank because the employer can, using the noncompete, stop the worker from working for another employer, while banks cannot expropriate a worker's human capital—a point that Becker's analysis of human capital overlooked.

While Rubin and Shedd's argument is logically coherent, an odd feature of it has been overlooked. One normally assumes that banks and other specialized credit institutions would lend money to people so that they can purchase training; indeed, that is quite common for higher education, and this assumption also motivated Becker's expectation that workers would obtain their own financing (presumably from banks) for general training. The only reason that employers take on this function in Rubin and Shedd's model is that banks and other creditors are not legally permitted to take a security interest in a person's human capital. A bank cannot obtain a court order blocking a defaulting debtor from taking a job. The reason is the same as the reason for the abolition of debtors' prison: the risk that people will be unable to work and support themselves and their families is too high, as is the risk that a creditor could use its leverage over the debtor in abusive ways.[28] But if that is all true, it is far from clear why an employer should be given the power that the bank is deprived of.

Rubin and Shedd's theory is really a theory of arbitrage, a theory about how employers use their control over workers to evade otherwise general legal restrictions on collateralizing human capital. If the logic of their argument is correct, those legal restrictions should be eliminated altogether so that specialized creditors like banks can fund investments in general human capital backed up by the right to prohibit workers from taking high-paying jobs if they fail to repay the loan, rather than argue that only employers should be spared them. But these legal restrictions reflect moral and humanitarian considerations, including worries about creating a permanent caste of unemployable people. Perhaps for this reason, while Rubin and Shedd's analysis is the standard citation for the investment theory and remains influential in the academic literature, it has made little impression on the courts.[29]

Asset theories. Employers frequently own a class of intangible assets that employees can easily expropriate or destroy, or technically, whose value is complementary to human capital.[30] Two such assets are frequently identified: trade secrets and customer relationships.

A trade secret is an asset in the sense of information that a firm uses to increase the quality of its products or reduce the cost of production. Firms frequently invest considerable resources to generate and protect trade secrets. They keep the information secret because if competitors get hold of it and use it, the originator of the trade secret will lose the return on its investment. The law extends significant protection to trade secrets on the theory that without such protection, firms would underinvest in innovation.

A major problem for firms that possess trade secrets is that trade secrets have value only to the extent that employees use them in production, which of course means that employees, or some of them, have access to them. And that means that an employee who learns trade secrets can sell them to other firms. Such thefts of trade secrets are illegal, and violators can be punished severely. But a more difficult problem arises when an employee who possesses trade secrets quits and goes to work for a competitor. Now it may be difficult to identify a theft because the employee may simply rely on her knowledge of those trade secrets while improving the production processes of the new employer. There may not be an easily identifiable "transfer" of the secrets from one person to another. To address this problem, the law allows the original employer to use a noncompete to block employees in possession of trade secrets from working for competitors. The noncompete thus helps employers fill a gap in the enforceability of trade secret law.

The customer relationship is another asset. A firm interacts with the outside world through its employees, but it retains a separate identity. The owners of the firm want its identity or "brand" to be associated in the customers' mind with the products or services it sells. The firm will devote resources to build up this association, using advertising, trade dress, trademarks, and other devices. The problem for the firm, as in the case with trade secrets, is that it must build up this association through its employees, who might be willing to disrupt it. Consider, for example, the employee who contacts, negotiates with, and makes a sale to a customer. Over time, the customer may come to trust the employee rather than the firm on whose behalf she acts. The "goodwill" that the firm enjoys with respect to the customer thus may be gradually transferred to the employee. That employee will then become more valuable for a competing firm, which can offer the employee a higher wage for, in effect, a transfer of that goodwill. To protect itself from the loss of the value of the customer relationship asset, the original employer may use a noncompete.[31]

Both the investment theory and the asset theory assume that labor markets are "frictionless," or at least lacking in sufficient friction—meaning that employees can too easily move from employer to employer. The problem arises for the employer when the employee moves to a competing employer. If employees stayed with their original employers, then those employers would not worry about losing their investments in training or intangible assets. Employers see noncompetes as a necessary means for increasing friction that would otherwise be insufficient to protect their interests. But there are grounds for skepticism about this premise. As we have seen, frictions abound in labor markets.

Moreover, training in general human capital does take place in the absence of noncompetes.[32] Among other things, the incumbent employer's superior information about the employees it trains gives it bargaining advantages over outside employers who may want to hire them away. This information advantage gives the employer the ability to retain employees by offering them higher wages than competing employers can; it supplies the friction that is needed to protect investment in employees.[33] Evidence suggests this information asymmetry and other natural frictions account for substantial investments in general training, including, for example, the apprenticeship system in Germany. In light of this natural friction that arises in the employment relationship, it seems doubtful that employers need the additional friction supplied by a noncompete.

If real-world labor market frictions often prevent employees from switching jobs, then these frictions should also enable employers to invest in general human capital and intangible assets like goodwill and trade secrets. A noncompete is necessary only to the extent that those frictions fall short. The benefit of a noncompete should thus be understood in marginal terms.

By enabling an employer to invest in training or intangible assets, a noncompete produces a benefit that can accrue to various different groups. If the product market is competitive, the employer will pass on the lower production costs enabled by the noncompete to consumers in the form of lower prices. If not, the noncompete will benefit the employer's shareholders, who recover the cost savings in the form of higher profits.

A noncompete will have more complex effects on compensation for the firm's workers. If the noncompete enables investments that improve the productivity of the workers, then normally their wages will increase as well.[34] However, the noncompete also deprives workers of outside opportunities, which both weakens the bargaining power of workers and deprives workers of possibly higher-paying jobs with competing employers. The net effect on workers will depend on the structure of the labor market and the nature of jobs offered by competing employers. I will address the net effects below.

The empirical literature on the effects of noncompetes is in its infancy, but it contains a few suggestive results. Mark Garmaise uses a data set of executives in large public firms in the United States.[35] He found that 70.2% of firms bound their executives with noncompetes. To test the effect of the noncompetes, he used an index of the legal enforceability of noncompetes across states, and also examined three states in which major legal changes in enforceability occurred during the time period of the data set. He found that greater enforceability of the law reduced employee mobility between firms, as one would expect, but reduced capital investment per employee instead of increased investment, as Rubin and Shedd's theory would predict.

However, in a paper that uses a larger and more diverse data set (of 52 million workers) and a similar research strategy, Jessica Jeffers found that greater legal enforceability of noncompetes increases employers' investment in their employees in a way that appears to be economically as well as statistically significant.[36]

Evan Starr also found that an increase in noncompete enforcement produces an increase in firm-sponsored training.[37] Using national survey data, he found that employees receive 14% more training in states that enforce noncompetes (at an "average" level) relative to states that do not. Workers in certain industries may receive greater benefits from noncompetes than others. Other studies also found some evidence of a link between noncompetes and various measures of investment.[38]

Unfortunately, these studies are no more than suggestive because of data limitations. It is also hard to interpret the results because variation in the legal enforceability of noncompetes across states does not necessarily equate to variation in the *use* of noncompetes by employers. Researchers have not been able to link investment decisions to specific workers based on whether they have signed a noncompete.

6.3. The Social Costs of Noncompetes

Harm to incumbent workers. A noncompete creates a cost for the employee by requiring her to continue working with the incumbent employer despite a superior offer from an outside employer, to stop working, to work in a different industry, or to work in another part of the country. While some employees can avoid the full extent of the hardship by continuing to work with their original employers— and forgoing a higher wage or better conditions elsewhere—some noncompetes apply to workers who are fired or laid off. Whatever the case, the employee incurs what I will call an "ex post cost"—ex post because it occurs after she signs the contract and begins work.

Some commentators and judges believe that the ex post cost should be disregarded—not treated as a harm at all—because employees will be compensated ex ante for the cost unless a bargaining failure occurs, in which case the contract should be voided under doctrines of contract law that protect parties from coercion and misinformation.[39] To understand this argument, suppose an employer and worker negotiate a contract in which the employee is paid $100,000 per year and is free to work for competitors upon termination. The employer then proposes that a noncompete be added to the contract. If the worker is rational and informed, she will demand a wage premium to compensate her for the expected "hardship" cost of the noncompete—the probability of being deprived of a higher wage from another employer. If the noncompete deprives the employee of, say, a 10% probability of being paid $150,000 by another employer, then the employee will require at least a $5,000 wage premium. Thus, if she ends up enduring the ex post cost, she has been compensated ex ante.

The argument is familiar from an analogous debate about workplace safety. A dangerous job creates the risk of injury and loss of work, and this risk can be seen as akin to the risk of unemployment (or continued employment with the original employer) created by a noncompete but with the additional harm of the injury itself. A large literature confirms that workers demand a wage premium for the more dangerous job,[40] though it is unclear whether the wage premium fully compensates the worker in an actuarial sense. Thus, one might assume that noncompetes are accompanied by wage premiums that compensate the worker for the risk that she will be unable to work for a period or will be required to remain in or take a less desirable job.

However, the empirical literature on noncompetes shows that workers and employers rarely bargain over noncompetes.[41] Workers often do not learn about noncompetes until after they start their job, or even until they threaten to quit and find a new job. It is theoretically possible that employers might seek a competitive advantage in the labor market by informing job applicants that other employers engage in these practices and offering to compensate employees for signing noncompetes, thus forcing competitors to do so as well. But the evidence suggests otherwise. As I discuss below, workers do *not* on average receive a wage premium for agreeing to noncompetes.

Harm to third parties. Noncompetes also harm parties who are not involved in the contract between the employer and the employee. To see why, imagine that an employee produces value of $100 (per hour) with the original employer. An outside employer could produce $120 if it employed the employee. Assume that the employee is indifferent between the two employers. Thus, the employee generates more social value if employed by the second employer than if employed by the incumbent employer. But the noncompete prohibits the outside employer from hiring the employee, resulting in social waste.[42]

One might respond that the outside employer and the incumbent employer should be able to negotiate around the noncompete. The outside employer could offer the incumbent employer an amount between $100 and $120 per hour to release the employee from the noncompete.

But there are two problems with this argument. First, renegotiation is vulnerable to bargaining failure. Standard models of bargaining suggest that when (as is almost always the case) bargainers do not know how much the other side values a deal, some bargains will fail and others will be delayed, in both cases resulting in a social cost.

Second, the incumbent employer may refuse to release the worker from the noncompete if it has labor market power that is threatened by the outside employer. Consider, for example, a scenario in which there are economies of scale in employment: per-person labor productivity increases with the number of employees. An employer may seek to deprive its labor-market competitors of the minimum-size labor force necessary to compete in the labor market. The employer thus maintains or enhances its labor market power, enabling it to suppress wages.[43]

This threat to competition can be seen more easily with an example. Imagine a labor market that extends over a county in a rural area. Let us suppose that 100 trained nurses reside in that county. Fifty of them currently work at the single hospital in the area, while the other 50 are either unemployed or employed in other markets that do not exploit their training.

The hospital owner worries that another hospital may be established in the county, offering competition both in the product market (for medical services) and in the labor market (for nurses, doctors, physician's assistants, laboratory technicians, and other specialized personnel). Assume further that a hospital can operate profitably only if it employs at least 50 nurses. (Similar assumptions could be made about other positions.) To block entry, the incumbent hospital hires a few additional (unneeded) nurses and subjects all its nurses to noncompetes of two years. This means that the new hospital cannot enter the market unless it either waits two years while in the meantime paying nurses to quit and remain unemployed for those two years or imports additional nurses from other locations.[44]

Clearly, the incumbent hospital can construct a significant entry barrier.[45] Even if the nurses employed by the incumbent hospital demand a significant wage premium in return for agreeing to noncompetes, this cost will be small relative to the anticompetitive benefits reaped by the incumbent hospital in multiple markets. Note that this entry barrier will harm not only the labor market for nurses but also all the other labor markets from which the hospital draws (including doctors) because a new employer is foreclosed. Moreover, the entry barrier will harm the product market for medical services. Nor can such a noncompete be blamed on bargaining failure. In perfect bargaining conditions, the employer and employee would split the rents extracted from third-party workers in multiple labor markets whose wages are suppressed because of lower competition for their labor, and from consumers who overpay for medical services because of the absence of product market competition.

In sum, a noncompete may cause harm to (1) workers in the labor market to which the employees subject to the noncompete belong, (2) other labor markets that the employer draws from, and (3) the product market that the employer sells into. All of these harms can exist even if a wage premium compensates the employee subject to the noncompete for her expected ex post costs.

Empirical research on the magnitude of the costs. The evidence suggests that noncompetes reduce wages. Starr found that wages were 4% higher in states that do not enforce noncompetes than in states with the mean level of enforceability.[46] A study by Natarajan Balasubramanian and coauthors similarly found that employees in nonenforcement states—including tech employees in Hawaii after a 2015 law banned noncompetes for tech workers—earn 4%–5% higher wages than employees in mean-enforcement states.[47] Garmaise's study of executive compensation found that a shift to a stricter enforcement state reduced executive compensation growth by 8.2%.[48] In a study limited to the impact of noncompetes on the wages of low-skill workers—who, according to economic theory, should be affected least by noncompetes because markets for low-skill labor are supposedly competitive—Michael

Lipsitz and Evan Starr found that a 2007 law in Oregon that banned noncompetes for workers with wages below the family median wage increased wages by 2%–3% for the average worker, meaning, of course, that the noncompetes originally reduced wages by that amount.[49] Because only a fraction of Oregon low-wage workers were subject to noncompetes at the time, the actual effect on such workers could have been as high as 14%–21% of their wages. Another study, by Matthew Johnson, Kurt Lavetti, and Lipsitz, uses a larger data set covering all changes in noncompete law in all states from 1991 and 2014 and similarly finds that an increase in enforcement of noncompetes from the 10th to the 90th percentile is associated with a 3%–4% decrease in earnings, suggesting that a ban on noncompetes could increase earnings nationwide by as much as 7%.[50]

Several studies also examine the effects of noncompetes on competition and entrepreneurial activities. Starr and his colleagues found that noncompete enforcement decreases the creation of "spinout" firms— firms founded by employees who leave their previous employer to start a new firm.[51] They found that a standard deviation increase in their measure of state law enforceability results in a 28.7% decline in new spinout firm formation.[52] Jeffers found a 12% decline in the creation of new "knowledge sector" firms following an increase in noncompete enforcement.[53] Sampsa Samila and Olav Sorenson found that venture capital was more effective at generating firms and jobs in a state that did not enforce noncompetes than in a state that did.[54] Hyo Kang and Lee Fleming found that when Florida increased enforceability of noncompetes in 1996, large firms moved to or were established in the state at a greater rate than small firms, resulting in more large-firm employment, and hence higher labor market concentration.[55] If noncompetes deter firm entry, incumbent firms benefit from reduced competition.[56]

Finally, evidence also indicates that noncompetes reduce employee mobility. Various studies find that as state law enforcement of noncompetes increases, the probability that employees switch jobs declines and tenure length at a given job increases, particularly for tech workers.[57] Noncompetes even reduce mobility in states where they are not enforceable because workers mistakenly believe that the noncompete clause is enforceable.[58] Reduction in mobility is not necessarily socially costly because workers may be adequately compensated for losing opportunities to switch jobs. But job mobility has macroeconomic benefits that employers and workers do not internalize. When workers can easily leave employers, the economy can more smoothly adjust to shocks. Job mobility has declined substantially over the past several decades.[59] If the growth of noncompetes has played a role in this broader trend, that is another reason for concern.

The research on noncompetes is at an early stage, and the findings should be interpreted cautiously because of data limitations and the difficulties of untangling causation. Moreover, while the research establishes that noncompetes reduce wages, it does not identify the relative impact of the two pathways we have discussed. It is possible that noncompetes suppress wages because workers who sign them do not demand a wage premium—because of ignorance or some other factor. It is also possible that noncompetes suppress wages because they block firms from entering labor markets and competing for workers.

6.4. Antitrust and Noncompetes

In a competitive market, wages should increase when noncompetes are added to employment contracts. Because the employee's mobility is reduced, the employer must compensate her. As Rubin and Shedd put it, "If an employer places a restrictive clause in an employment contract, he will reduce the supply of potential employees and thus pay a higher wage to those persons who nonetheless choose to work for him."[60] The empirical research contradicts this claim: wages generally decline rather than increase in states that enforce or strictly enforce noncompetes.

The most plausible explanation for this finding is that labor markets are frequently not competitive, as this book has argued. Noncompetes can further reduce labor market competition by deterring entry. Recall from the hospital example that a firm can deter entry by requiring its employees to sign noncompetes, even compensating them if necessary. This strategy will not work if the labor market is competitive. If many employers exist, then they will all benefit from entry deterrence, but that also means that they will be inclined to free-ride on each other rather than incur the cost of paying a worker to sign a noncompete. But in fact, most labor markets are highly concentrated. And even when labor markets are relatively competitive, so that noncompetes are associated with wage premiums when they are initially introduced, the spread of noncompetes may eventually cause market concentration by deterring entry, and ultimately cause harm in aggregate.

None of this would matter much if noncompetes were used infrequently. But as Starr and his colleagues have demonstrated, noncompetes are extremely common. The authors found that 38.1% of employees in the U.S. labor market have signed a noncompete at some point in their lives, and 18.1% were subject to a noncompete agreement in 2014.[61] Among lower-income workers, 34.7% of employees without bachelor's degrees were subject to noncompetes at some point in their lives, compared to 45.4% of employees with at least a bachelor's degree.[62] Another survey, using a different methodology, found that between 27.8 and 46.5% of the private-sector workforce is subject to a noncompete.[63] Widespread, indiscriminate use of noncompetes of this sort likely erects entry barriers.

When a plaintiff alleges that a noncompete violates antitrust law, the first step should be to identify all the markets in which the noncompete may cause harm. As we have seen, there are three types of markets: direct labor markets, indirect labor markets, and product markets.

The direct labor market, which I discussed in the previous section, is the market for the labor of the worker who is subject to the noncompete. Suppose, for example, that a primary care physician in Toledo is subject to a noncompete. The direct labor market is primary care physicians in Toledo. The noncompete reduces competition in this labor market by preventing an outside employer from hiring away this physician.

The indirect labor market is any other market (or markets) for the labor of workers who may not be hired because a firm cannot obtain economies of scale as a result of the noncompete. For example, imagine that a hospital chain cannot enter Toledo because it cannot hire enough primary care physicians as a result of their commitments to noncompetes. The failure to enter harms not only the (direct) labor market for primary care physicians. It also harms the (indirect) labor markets for emergency room physicians, nurses, physician's assistants, and other hospital personnel and even harms indirect labor markets for less specialized personnel, including administrative assistants and custodians (unless those markets are highly competitive). These indirect labor markets will also be more concentrated than they would be if entry occurred.

The product market is the market in which the excluded employer sells products or services. In the example, the relevant product market is hospital or medical services. Because the hospital cannot enter the Toledo medical services market, that product market is more concentrated than it would be otherwise. This is also an effect of the noncompete.

6.5. How Can Noncompetes Be Challenged under Antitrust Law?

Section 1 of the Sherman Act applies to any contract in restraint of trade. A noncompete falls cleanly under Section 1 because it is a contractual obligation with just that effect. The traditional problem for plaintiffs is that courts apply the rule of reason to noncompetes. Under the rule of reason, the plaintiff must show that the defendant possesses market power and that the noncompete measurably reduces competition.[64] While commentators and courts disagree about how burdensome the rule of reason is as a general matter, in the noncompete setting the burden appears to be high. The problem may be that when a single employee challenges a single noncompete, the effect of the noncompete on wages will be lost in statistical noise. This may explain why no challenge to a noncompete under Section 1 has been successful.

It is possible that a more sensitive use of the rule of reason could cure this problem. But the better view is that the application of the rule of reason to noncompetes is a mistake. Some courts have suggested that the rule of reason approach should be used for restraints when they are "vertical" or "ancillary" to a valid contract.[65] The noncompete is thus treated as similar to an exclusive dealing agreement, which is also evaluated under the rule of reason.[66] These categories are unhelpful. A typical vertical restraint involves a transaction between two firms at different locations on the distribution chain—say, a manufacturer and a wholesaler, or a wholesaler and a retailer. For example, a retailer might agree not to buy products from a competitor of the wholesaler. Or, to use the monopsony case, a supplier might agree not to sell to a competitor of a manufacturer. The worker is not the same as a supplier. While both a worker and a supplier provide an "input" (labor, goods, services), the worker is subject to the control of the employer, while the supplier is an independent contractor. Because independent contractors deal with multiple buyers, while the worker deals with a single buyer of her labor, workers are more vulnerable if the employer threatens to stop buying, that is, to fire her. Indeed, the major source of employers' monopsony power is the worker's inability to hold out for a higher wage by credibly threatening to stop working altogether—a problem that a supplier does not have.

The ancillary restraint category is meant to identify restraints of trade that are justified as part of a larger transaction that is on the whole procompetitive. An example is the noncompete ancillary to the sale of a business. While a "naked" noncompete between two businesses is per se illegal, an ancillary noncompete may be lawful when the owner of one business sells it to another so that the buyer can be sure the original owner will not set up a competitor that destroys the goodwill of the first business.[67] However, the ancillary restraint idea is based on the assumption that ancillary restraints are on average procompetitive rather than anticompetitive. As we have seen, the empirical research suggests that employee noncompetes are on average anticompetitive.

Commentators and courts do not put much stock in these categories in any event. The better view is that the law applies the rule of reason to transactions that are not likely to be anticompetitive, and it declares per se illegal those transactions that are likely to be anticompetitive. The category of "quick look" is sometimes used for transactions that fall into the middle.[68] Or to put the matter differently, the burden imposed on the plaintiff decreases as the risk of anticompetitive harm increases, based on an empirical assessment of the way the various transactions are typically used.

The empirical literature suggests that noncompetes typically cause anticompetitive harm in the form of lower wages for workers. This suggests that they should be regarded as presumptively illegal—possibly under the per se standard or otherwise under the quick look standard. While the analytic framework for the quick look standard remains disputed, at a minimum it suggests that courts should not demand proof of market power and should be more skeptical of the employer's business justification than under the rule of reason. It is, of course, possible that the rule of reason could remain the right approach if courts are sufficiently receptive to the empirical literature and do not burden plaintiffs with an excessive obligation to show market power. A rule-of-reason approach that shifted the burden to the defendant once the plaintiff showed that a noncompete prevented him or her from moving to a higher-paying job would, for all intents and purposes, be the same as a quick look. The doctrinal pigeonhole is less important than recognition of the underlying empirical reality.

Using any of these approaches, an employee subject to a noncompete would nearly always have a prima facie Section 1 claim. For those who prefer a more incremental change in the law, one could imagine a more moderate approach that limited a prima facie case to broader rather than narrower noncompetes. For example, antitrust law could import the common law standard, so that a prime facie claim exists only when a noncompete is excessive under the common law—lacks a protectable interest, for example, or is unnecessarily broad for an asserted protectable interest, or involves low-skill labor. The burden would then shift to the employer, who would be able to escape liability if it could provide a procompetitive business justification that outweighs any adverse effects on its workers.

In product-market cases, defendants are allowed to rebut prima facie claims by showing that the purportedly anticompetitive behavior actually advances competition or has some other legitimate justification. A key requirement in these cases is that the benefits occur in the same market that is allegedly harmed by the anticompetitive behavior. In typical product-market cases, the efficiency gain must generate lower prices for consumers despite the loss of competition. Higher returns for shareholders will not justify a merger that results in higher prices for consumers even if in aggregate social wealth increases.

Similarly, an employer could defend itself against a challenge to a noncompete by arguing that the noncompete is necessary to protect an investment in training or to preserve goodwill, trade secrets, or customer lists. But the employer would be required to prove rather than merely assert these defenses, and prove that the noncompete generates higher rather than lower wages (which is not a requirement of the common law). To do so, an employer could show that in similar markets where employers do not use noncompetes, they provide less training to workers or entrust them with fewer intangible assets, and as a result those workers receive lower wages. The employer would also need to show that it could not have used less restrictive means of obtaining the same result. For example, an employer's defense would fail if the evidence demonstrated that, in the absence of a noncompete, the employer would have given the same training (or was able to preserve goodwill, trade secrets, or customer lists, etc.).

Where a noncompete harms product markets, the employer could defend itself, as in standard product-market cases, by showing that prices fall rather than rise because productivity gains are passed on to consumers. However, where a noncompete harms indirect labor markets, a defense may well be impossible. If a hospital blocks entry by rivals by ensnaring doctors in noncompetes, and as a result it is able to underpay lab technicians, then the competitive harm will not be offset in the lab technician labor market. The noncompete would be illegal.

Courts could look at other aspects of the market when evaluating an employer's claimed business justification. The following factors would be a strike against employers:

- The productivity benefits depreciate quickly. The employer can recover the investment in the short term by requiring the worker to work concurrently with the training, rather than structuring the employment relationship as one in which a long period of initial training without work is followed by another long period of work without training.
- The employer enjoys information advantages with respect to the productivity effects of training for a particular worker. These information advantages give the employer bargaining power vis-à-vis competing employers.
- The labor market is concentrated. Because few employers compete for the worker who receives the training, the probability that the incumbent employer will fail to recover its investment is low.
- Search costs are high. Because workers can find a new job only at great cost, turnover is low, and the employer is likely to recover its investment even without a noncompete.

- Jobs that are classified the same almost always differ across employers because of subtle differences in culture, amenities, location, and other factors. Job differentiation leads to low turnover, as a result of which a noncompete may be unnecessary.
- The employer's dominance over the product market or over other labor markets is facilitated by a noncompete imposed on a worker in the labor market in question.

Antitrust law's failure to regulate noncompetes is puzzling in light of the aggressive stance that the law takes toward no-poaching agreements, which per se violate Section 1.[69] The confusion lies in the crude doctrinal categories used by antitrust law: noncompetes are "vertical" (agreements between parties who do not compete with each other) rather than "horizontal" (agreements between parties who do compete), and in antitrust law horizontal agreements are suspect because they directly reduce competition, while vertical agreements are not. But that is a generalization and not always true. While a noncompete is vertical rather than horizontal, the anticompetitive effect of a noncompete is greater than that of a no-poaching agreement. A noncompete prohibits employees from working for *any* competitor of their employer, whereas a no-poaching agreement prevents employment only by the competitor or competitors who signed the agreement. While a no-poaching agreement can, of course, have multiple parties, an agreement with a large number of parties is difficult to orchestrate and enforce and to keep secret from the authorities.

There are two possible reasons why noncompetes might be treated more leniently than no-poaching agreements. First, because the noncompete is made with the employee, the employer must compensate the employee—at least if the employee is sophisticated enough to demand compensation—for agreeing to the noncompete. If the employee is compensated, then the employer is sharing some of the rents with the employee—who is effectively a member of an anticompetitive conspiracy—rather than keeping them for itself. Thus, it might be more expensive to maintain a large labor market share using noncompetes than using no-poaching agreements among employers. However, this argument seems backward. Most employees do not bargain over noncompetes, and many employees are not even aware of them. By contrast, an employer must find, bargain with, agree with, and monitor the agreement with other employers when it enters into no-poaching agreements.

Second, it might be argued that noncompetes can be justified when they encourage firms to invest in training or in intangible assets, whereas no such justification is available for no-poaching agreements. However, no-poaching agreements could be justified in the same way. If an employer is justified in blocking a worker from moving to competitors, it should not matter whether the employer uses a noncompete or a no-poaching agreement. The problem for the employer is simply that the employee might move to a competitor, and noncompetes and no-poaching agreements are equally good responses to this problem. The different treatment of the two arrangements merely reflects legal convention—the disinclination to allow antitrust defendants to provide justifications for naked horizontal agreements—and not economic theory or evidence.

PART III

Beyond Antitrust

7

The Limits of Antitrust

7.1. Labor Markets versus Product Markets (Again)

I have argued that antitrust law is a useful tool for correcting power imbalances in labor markets. Even without reform, antitrust law offers opportunities that private litigants and government officials have failed to exploit. With even modest reform, antitrust law could be significantly more valuable for countering wage suppression. But there are limits to antitrust law. Stricter merger review, for example, would reduce the rate of further labor market concentration but not unwind past mergers; even strict merger review may not be able to stop long-term trends toward concentration caused by growing economies of scale and other factors. It is unlikely that courts would break up large labor market monopsonists under the antitrust law, and even if they did, this would not likely have much impact, since labor market concentration is mostly a local phenomenon. And, within limits, firms can locate plants in sparely populated areas in order to avoid labor market competition. Antitrust law is unlikely to block such behavior because the additional jobs, even if low-paying, are on balance beneficial to the local labor force.

As in the product market case, some increased labor monopsony has probably been caused by trade and technological factors unrelated to mergers and other types of anticompetitive behavior that can be targeted by antitrust law. Efraim Benmelech and his coauthors show that exposure to Chinese trade shocks resulted in increased labor market concentration in manufacturing, lowering wages in exposed labor markets (particularly nonunionized ones).[1] Many tech firms owe their market dominance to network effects. It would have been difficult for antitrust authorities to stop Google and Facebook from achieving product market dominance because they gained most of their early market share by offering products and services that customers wanted. Similarly, on the labor market side, firms like Uber have exploited advances in technology that have enabled them to isolate and monitor workers and circumvent legal protections like minimum wage laws; they have not needed to merge with other firms in order to obtain this labor market power.

But there is a further problem for labor markets, which is that they are highly fragmented—far more so than most product markets. The reason is that people are less mobile than goods, with the result that labor market areas are typically (though not always) smaller than product market areas. To understand this point, consider, for example, the merger of two big farm equipment manufacturers. The market for farm equipment is national in scope,[2] and hence an agency or court that evaluates the merger can focus on that single national market. To evaluate labor market effects, by contrast, one must identify the location of the factories of the two firms, which may be scattered throughout the country (or world). In some labor market areas, the merger may result in factory shutdowns, in others not. One then must evaluate all aspects of the local labor market—such as whether other employers, including employers in different industries, offer comparable jobs. And one must take into account the different types of workers in each factory; for example, line workers and IT workers belong in different labor markets. While some product markets are fragmented in this way, the problem for labor market antitrust is that fragmentation is pervasive if not universal.

Next, consider the problem of search frictions. These frictions can create market power in product markets as well as labor markets. Consumers who have trouble searching for substitutes—say, for their cell phone plan because of the complexity of the product and the difficulty of comparison—are subject to product market power from sellers. But not all products are complex or otherwise involve search frictions. A huge range of products are simple commodities—in many cases easily evaluated (like furniture), in other cases made comparable thanks to private and government market interventions that have produced standard types and grades and resulted in disclosures like nutrition information and safety records. Even for more complex products and services, an enormous intermediary market of advisers, like Consumer Reports, have emerged to reduce the cost of search.

In contrast, search costs in labor markets are high. Similar-seeming jobs often involve enormous variation. For example, the job description of a lawyer at a law firm might be "complex litigation" or "complex commercial litigation." But lawyers with this job description do very different things at different firms because different firms have different cases, divide tasks among litigators differently, and—of course—have different lawyers, which will affect the various interpersonal relationships that are involved in any litigation. As in the product market case, intermediaries—headhunters—have arisen to help reduce search frictions. But these intermediary markets are themselves opaque. The search frictions give employers bargaining power over their workers to a far greater extent than exists in product markets. While new companies like Glassdoor, which aggregate employee ratings of a variety of jobs and employers, may help reduce these search frictions, progress remains limited.

Conventional antitrust enforcement would not address wage suppression caused by search costs or job differentiation except in unusual cases where it can be shown that firms took deliberate steps to increase search costs and job differentiation for anticompetitive purposes. Imaginably, a firm could be liable for antitrust violations if it tried to forbid workers to search for new jobs. But high search costs may simply be a feature of a labor market, for example, because jobs involve complex and hard-to-compare tasks and amenities.

Similar points can be made about job differentiation. This source of labor market power is, like search costs, related to the complexity of the work relationship. Search costs are the result of information asymmetries over the wages available, while job differentiation refers to variation in the preferences of workers over different types of jobs. Some law firms have highly intense and competitive cultures; others don't. These differences appeal to different types of lawyers. Thus, an apparently large labor market, such as litigators, turns out to be smaller: intense and nonintense litigators. And then there are further types of differentiation as well, like case types; some people prefer antitrust cases, and others prefer employment cases, and many law firms specialize accordingly. Here again, we can think of product-market analogies, but they are rare rather than pervasive. Some airlines differentiate themselves by offering better service and others by offering low prices. Insurance companies also offer complicated different features in insurance contracts. But there seems to be natural limits on this type of differentiation—perhaps because more complex differentiation confuses consumers or because entrants can attract customers from incumbents by offering simpler products. Moreover, because work is such an important part of people's life, people are naturally concerned about even minor aspects of it, whereas most products—housing is probably the only exception—add relatively little value to one's life.[3]

Like search costs, job differentiation poses significant challenges to antitrust law. When employers differentiate jobs, they can nearly always claim that they are merely giving their workers what those workers want or providing attractive positions to people who may be unsatisfied with their jobs at rival firms. Thus, job differentiation can easily be seen as procompetitive. And job differentiation may also arise naturally as firms compete for workers with different workplace tastes. It would be difficult for courts to distinguish this type of natural job differentiation from job differentiation that occurs as a conscious strategy to suppress wages.

7.2. Evidence

In this section, I draw on an article written with Suresh Naidu to show how to think about the relative contributions of competition and noncompetition sources of labor monopsony.[4] In the article, we use a model of imperfect competition that allows for both concentration- and non-concentration-based sources of monopsony. Firms compete for workers with an eye to what other firms are doing: as the number of employers declines, wages decline as well. Using existing estimates of concentration and aggregate and firm-specific labor supply elasticities, we can calculate how much monopsony power would result if concentration were eliminated. The results of the exercise are in Figure 7.1.

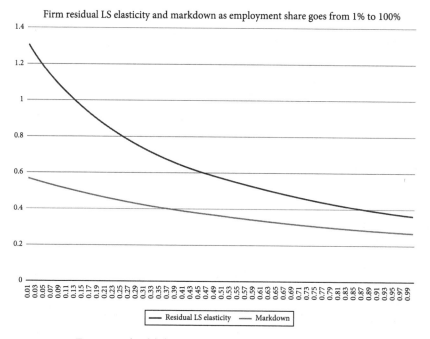

Firm residual LS elasticity and markdown as employment share goes from 1% to 100%

Residual LS elasticity   Markdown

FIGURE 7.1. Firm residual labor supply elasticity and markdown as labor market concentration rises from 1% to 100%

The graph shows that both firm-specific labor supply elasticity and the resulting wage (markdown) decline as concentration increases, as one would expect. But most of the harmful effect is the result of nonconcentration sources of labor monopsony. Even if perfect competition prevails, workers are paid less than 60% of the competitive rate. To see the limits of antitrust law, imagine that the law were able to convert perfectly concentrated markets into perfectly competitive markets. While wages would more than double, they would not increase beyond the 60% threshold. And, realistically, antitrust law will produce a more incremental effect on market concentration, and thus an incremental impact on wages.

Antitrust law can do much good for workers in concentrated markets. But to make more progress with labor monopsony, we need other tools as well. Those tools are the subject of the next chapter.

8

Employment and Labor Law: Old and New Directions

IN LIGHT OF THE limits of antitrust law, what other legal tools can be used to address labor monopsony? Solutions can be divided into three categories: reduce labor market power by increasing competition; impose either internal governance mechanisms or wage/benefit standards that prevent firms from exercising their labor market power; and ameliorate the inefficiencies resulting from the exercise of labor market power. Table 8.1 offers a summary of conventional labor policies and how they address monopsony. In each case, I show how the regulation in question may address the various problems I identify, the limits of the regulation, and the costs that the regulation may impose on the economy. Unfortunately, these regulatory approaches are often weak or limited. Indeed, some of them may in fact exacerbate rather that ameliorate the monopsony distortion.

Antitrust law helps workers and increases output by penalizing firms that use anticompetitive methods—above all, firms that concentrate labor markets by merging and firms that collude with each other by entering no-poaching agreements and the like. The law thus raises residual supply elasticity—or, in other words, competition—which forces employers to bid up wages toward the competitive level. Antitrust law does not directly regulate wages, of course; wages increase as a result of the penalizing of anticompetitive behavior. Nor does antitrust law offset the distortions introduced into labor markets by labor monopsony—in the way that certain fiscal and related policies can, as we will see. Let

TABLE 8.1 Labor Market Policies and Margins of Monopsony Targeted

Policy	Raising Residual Supply Elasticity	Directly Setting Wages/ Compensation	Offsetting Distortion
Antitrust	Y	N	N
Wage mandates	N	Y	N
EITC/wage subsidy	N	N	Y
Mandatory benefits	?	Y	N
Job protection	?	N	N
Licensing	Y?	N	N
Training	Y?	N	Y
Job standardization	Y	N	N
Unions	Y	Y	N
Governance reforms	N	Y	N
Macroeconomic tightness	Y	N	Y

us now turn to other policy tools that can be used to counter labor monopsony.

8.1. Wage Regulation

A much-discussed response to the problem of wage suppression is the minimum wage or living wage law.[1] A minimum wage prohibits the employer from paying workers a wage below a certain level. Mandatory minimums in this spirit can be, and often are, applied to other aspects of work. For example, maximum hours laws limit the number of hours that workers can be required to work or require extra pay for hours above that limit. Laws that require employers to meet minimum health and safety standards have a similar effect. They prevent an employer from underproviding what is effectively in-kind compensation in the form of relatively safe or pleasant working conditions.

The standard criticism of minimum wage laws is that they will result in unemployment as employers fire workers to whom they must pay a wage greater than the workers' marginal revenue product. But this criticism assumes that labor markets are competitive. If labor monopsony prevails, a minimum wage law—if not too high—will raise wages without reducing employment. The more serious problem with minimum wage laws is that they can help only a small class of relatively poor people, workers who would otherwise be paid slightly less than the minimum wage, and not more deeply impoverished people or workers higher on the wage scale. When the monopsonistic wage level exceeds the minimum wage, minimum wage laws have no effect. If the wage is only a small part of the total compensation, or total compensation is fungible between wage and nonwage components, minimum wages alone will have a negligible effect. Moreover, the minimum wage must be carefully calibrated: if the wage level is set too high, then disemployment effects may be greater than the wage benefits, and employers may raise prices that end up being paid by the same workers whose wages are raised.[2] It may be difficult for governments to calibrate the minimum wage correctly. On the whole, uniform minimum wage laws can be only a small part of the response to wage suppression caused by monopsonistic competition.

A more thorough and flexible wage-mandate response to pervasive monopsony would be wage boards, which are used in Australia and in some U.S. states for some industries. Wage boards periodically set wage floors by industry, occupation, and location, using nonpartisan expert appointees (in the Australian case) or tripartite employer-worker-government commissions (in the U.S. case).[3]

8.2. Tax and Transfer Policies

It is well understood that the fiscal system solution to market power involves subsidizing the price paid by the firm. For example, the government could offer to pay a monopolist a subsidy for every unit sold, so that the monopolist voluntarily manufactures and sells the number of units that it would produce in a competitive market. Transposed to labor markets, the government would subsidize the wage. Standing alone, such a scheme would have unattractive distributive effects because it would benefit the corporation more than workers. But if a corporate tax on profits was coupled with a precisely tuned subsidy on wages, the gains from alleviating the monopsony distortion via a subsidy could be redistributed.

Under this approach, the government should apply the subsidy only to employers with monopsony power, and the extent of the subsidy should be a function of the degree of monopsony power. But the existence, and especially the degree, of labor market power is never self-evident. It is the domain of antitrust law in the first place to determine whether an employer has power in a labor market, and this fact-intensive inquiry seems to require lengthy hearings by courts.

A popular policy that has unanticipated consequences under monopsony is the Earned Income Tax Credit. The EITC subsidizes earnings of low-income households and is among the largest forms of redistribution in the United States. However, in monopsonized labor markets, the EITC can have perverse consequences. By increasing the effective (after-tax) wage earned by the worker, it encourages people to enter the labor market, enabling employers to pay a lower wage to the incumbent workers. While the EITC can mitigate the disemployment effects of monopsony, it will also transfer a share of those benefits to employers while reducing wages for incumbent workers.[4]

The policy mix for combating labor monopsony may involve unemployment insurance (UI). While a large literature considers the optimal level of UI in light of the insurance-incentives trade-off, little of this literature has accounted for the role of UI in blunting employer market power. For example, legitimate reasons to quit can allow a worker to exit employment into the UI system, putting some brakes on employer ability to exert monopsony power. However, almost all UI systems do not permit people who voluntarily quit to receive UI. As a result, the threat to quit based on UI payments will rarely be credible and so will not enhance the worker's bargaining power. This may account for why recent evidence has shown that within-firm increases in UI generosity do not lead to appreciably higher wages.[5] The enormous expansion of the UI system during the COVID pandemic may have altered the terms under which workers are eligible for UI, increasing its role as a possible counterweight to monopsony.[6]

8.3. Mandatory Benefits

Workers are protected by a range of laws that require employers to offer certain benefits to them. Federal mandates include workers compensation, safety and health requirements, family and medical leave requirements, and special treatments for veterans.[7] States also impose mandates. Illinois, for example, requires employers to give workers time for a meal if they continuously work 7.5 hours or more and prohibits employers from penalizing employees who miss work in order to vote or serve on a jury.[8] Mandates can be loosely defined as legally required in-kind transfers from the employer to the workers, where the workers attach or may attach an intrinsic value to the benefit.

These policies have often puzzled economists because they seem to substitute the government's judgment about the conditions of employment for the employee's own judgment as to what may be best for her. Consider, for example, a mandate that employers grant unpaid leave to workers who experience a family medical emergency. It would seem that if workers value unpaid leave of this type a sufficient amount, employers would grant it to them even in the absence of the mandate. The unpaid leave is simply an in-kind benefit—effectively, a kind of weak employer-supplied insurance policy.[9]

The logic is the same if the employer is a labor monopsonist. Indeed, it is possible that the labor monopsonist has stronger incentives than a nonmonopsonist to offer certain packages of benefits because the monopsonist will obtain a larger share of the marginal surplus from retained workers. To see why, imagine that the marginal worker (the one indifferent between working at this firm and the outside option) values amenities more than all the inframarginal workers (those who value working at the firm more than the outside option).[10] A monopsonist may have an incentive to offer a package of low wages and amenities that appeals to the marginal worker but is also transferring surplus from the inframarginal workers to the employer.[11] In such circumstances, labor market mandates, just like quality standards in product markets, may have a role to play in curbing the distortion in job design induced by monopsony.

The story is more complex if, as will usually be the case, the monopsonist has limited information about employees and potential hires.[12] Employers may use packages of wages and benefits to avoid adverse selection problems but that, from the social standpoint, are inefficient.[13] But a policy of mandating benefits in such circumstances does not have straightforward efficiency effects.

Further, to the extent that the cost of benefits is larger than the value workers attach to those benefits, mandates will act as a tax, and thus magnify the monopsony distortion, resulting in even lower employment and wages than in the competitive case. Mandates may not generally address labor monopsony power except in the limited case where the minimum wage is binding, and so the addition of a mandate has the effect of increasing the effective compensation of a low-income worker. Even here, however, raising the minimum wage would be the better remedy to the problem of labor monopsony, unless the wage is a small share of total compensation. Mandates do not address wage suppression caused by monopsony power.

8.4. Job Protection

In the United States, most jobs are at-will: the employer can fire the worker for any reason not specifically forbidden by law (such as racial discrimination). In one state, Minnesota, the law provides that employers may fire workers only "for cause." Under the for-cause standard, employers may fire workers only if they can prove that the workers are unable or unwilling to perform the job up to standards. In other countries, some workers have even more secure forms of tenure. Laws that put limits on termination of workers also typically prevent the employer from taking lesser forms of actions against workers, like reducing wages or even failing to make cost-of-living adjustments.

Job protection laws enjoy a great deal of support among legal academics who believe that employers use their power over workers in an arbitrary fashion. This view has been countered by economists who believe that employers who fire workers arbitrarily would put themselves at a competitive disadvantage in the labor market. The question for now is whether job protection laws could help counter labor monopsony. The answer is: maybe. In the simplest variant of the Burdett-Mortensen model of search, job protections could be understood as lowering the (exogenous) separations rate, and thus the tightness of the labor market (ratio of recruitment to separations rate) increases, moving the labor market closer to efficiency. Because fewer workers are fired, fewer are available to hire, and employers must compete more vigorously to hire those who remain. However, if employers lose profits because they cannot fire underperforming workers, then the employer reduction in recruitment effort may outweigh the reduction in the separation rate.

Job protection rules may reduce the bargaining power of employers by depriving them of the ability to fire a worker who refuses to accept a low wage or insists on a higher wage. But they do not help workers in concentrated labor markets: the initial wage will be set at the monopsony rate. At most, they help workers who obtain work at the market wage, or a relatively high wage, and then lose bargaining power as the labor market consolidates or the workers' outside options diminish for other reasons. These workers will be unable to obtain raises that they would receive in a competitive labor market.

Job protection also has negative consequences. Many economists worry that the job protection laws in some countries damage the macroeconomy by decreasing labor mobility and reducing employers' incentives to hire in the first place.

A weaker form of job protection comes in the form of notice requirements. The Worker Adjustment and Retraining Notification Act requires employers to give workers notice before laying them off. Notice benefits workers by enabling them to start their job searches while they are still being paid. Notice requirements may therefore enhance workers' bargaining power by reducing search costs, although perhaps only modestly.

8.5. Occupational Licensing

Many types of employment are subject to occupational licensing statutes. These statutes require people to undergo training and certification before offering services to the public. Traditional examples include lawyers and doctors, but in the past few decades the list of occupations that are subject to these rules has lengthened considerably and now includes (depending on the state) hairdressers, auto mechanics, financial advisers, civil engineers, electricians, and funeral directors, among many others.

The traditional justification for occupational licensing is quality control. If the government can screen out incompetent service providers, consumers will benefit. Many researchers are skeptical of this justification and have argued that the main effect of occupational licensing has been to erect entry barriers that raised prices for services, reduced supply, and benefited incumbents. Occupational licensing lowers the supply of labor to a given market, and thus raises wages of the licensed, lowers profits of firms (and raises prices to consumers), and lowers the wages of the unlicensed.

Unfortunately, occupational licensing also imposes a cost on people who want to enter the workforce in the first place since they must pay for training that may otherwise be unnecessary, as well as the fees for certifications. For this reason, occupational licensing may not on balance be a useful way to counter employer monopsony power.

It is possible that occupational licensing could help workers counter the labor monopsony power of employers if licensing makes the supply to the firm more elastic as well as lower. This could be the case if, for example, competing firms can more easily evaluate, and hence hire away, licensed workers than workers not subject to license—perhaps if the licensing process standardizes and makes more transparent worker quality. But this possibility has not been addressed in the empirical literature on licensing.

8.6. Government Subsidies, Including Training and Employment

Numerous government programs offer skills training for people. The U.S. government subsidizes student loans and offers tuition grants. States and local governments provide subsidized schooling, vocational training, and university training. Many programs help workers who have lost jobs. For example, the Department of Labor runs the Employment and Training Administration, which offers retraining programs to dislocated workers, among others. The Workforce and Innovation Opportunity Act, passed in 2014, provided additional resources for supporting and retraining people who have lost their jobs. States and local governments also offer numerous services to unemployed workers, including training and matching.

These programs offer benefits to ordinary people, but most of them do not address the problem of labor market power. Consider, for example, federal grants and loan subsidies for students who seek to attend college. In the absence of such benefits, people will either borrow in the private market or refrain from going to college. In the first case, the benefit is equal to the difference between the cost of borrowing in the private market and the cost of subsidized borrowing along with any grants. In the second case, the benefit is equal to the difference between future income that is obtained as a result of the college education (net of costs) and future income otherwise obtained. In both cases, the benefit is a transfer from taxpayers to the generally lower-income people who qualify for these programs. Employers may be benefited from the larger pool of qualified labor. Monopsonistic employers remain free to use their market power to suppress the wages of the people they hire. It is even possible that as the pool of trained workers increases, the workers lose bargaining power, which further enhances the bargaining power of monopsonistic employers, who thus obtain a larger share of the surplus generated by the government programs.

Insofar as worker and firm underinvestment in training is a symptom of excessive labor market power, policies to encourage training can mitigate the distortion. But without reducing the degree of monopsony power, the bulk of the returns from training will be captured by employers. Indeed, some of the enthusiasm for government training programs emanating from the private sector may be due to labor market power: monopsonists are always labor constrained and demand more and more skilled labor without wanting to raise wages or pay for training.

Some educational programs may, however, help counter labor market power. Job-retraining programs that teach relatively general skills may facilitate occupational mobility. To see why, imagine that a single meat-processing plant dominates the local labor market for meat-processing workers. Because the workers have few outside options if they are fired, the employer can suppress wages. Now imagine that the government offers job retraining for anyone who has been fired from a job. The program improves the value of the workers' outside option by enabling them to earn a higher income once they undergo the training after they have been fired. This should increase their bargaining power vis-à-vis the employer, who in turn should refrain from suppressing wages as much as it otherwise would. Note that this pathway for countering labor market power works by reducing search frictions for workers rather than by reducing market concentration or directly regulating the terms of employment.

Retraining programs, and other programs that help laid-off workers find new, well-paying jobs, could thus be a useful way to counter labor market power. But these programs also have many limitations. They are costly and will be justified only when the benefits for workers exceed those costs. It may also be difficult for the government to offer appropriate retraining programs. The government needs to be able to forecast the demand for the jobs for which training is needed and the willingness of workers to take those jobs and undergo training for them. This type of forecasting may be challenging.

8.7. Job Standardization

None of the proposals I have discussed addresses the problem of job differentiation, where labor market power arises because apparently similar jobs are actually quite different for workers because of variation in amenities across workplaces. The simplest amenity to think about is commute time: employers that are dispersed across residential locations have more market power than employers that occupy a dense central business district. Other amenities include shift flexibility, benefits, and corporate culture. This problem seems intractable because the variation of amenities may reflect the different preferences of workers, and employers would normally be justified in catering to different preferences. But the result is that employers can underpay workers who cannot find valued amenities in other workplaces.

At least as a theoretical matter, however, workers (and the economy) could benefit if labor market differentiation was deterred at the margin.[14] Unions have sometimes performed this function by standardizing jobs across firms within industries.[15] Nonwage characteristics of unionized jobs are very important to workers' preferences for unionization.[16] The law also plays a role in standardizing work. Minimum wage and maximum hours laws push employers to offer standard eight-hour workdays. This puts a limit on the duration of shifts, which in turn should reduce the variation across employers of this dimension of work. Government-mandated health and safety regulations should also reduce job differentiation by putting a floor under the health and safety conditions of any workplace. However, as far as I know, no study documents the job-differentiation effects of union practices and legal regulations on employer market power, likely because many of these regulations also come with mandated changes in wages, limiting the value of the exercise.

Some markets for services seem to be naturally standardized. Consider, for example, the services offered to households by plumbers, electricians, dry cleaners, locksmiths, carpenters, and other skilled workers. Because these workers typically sell services to numerous households, they are not subject to typical labor monopsony pressures. The law recognizes this distinction by classifying these workers as independent contractors and denying them the protections of employment and labor law—including, for example, minimum wage laws, and the right to unionize. The law apparently assumes that market competition protects these workers, and so legal protections are unnecessary or less necessary. In contrast, if a (say) plumber goes to work for a single firm like a hotel, the plumber is likely to be classified as an employee because the buyer of her services has more "control" (or labor market power) over her. I will return to this topic in chapter 9.

8.8. Support for Unions

Workers have historically turned to union organization to counter the labor market power of employers. Unionization deprives the employer of its main source of market power: the ability to set the wage. The evidence suggests that unions counter labor monopsony; for example, when a merger increases labor market concentration, wages fall less in unionized labor markets than in nonunionized labor markets.[17] However, unions are fragile organizations. They must maintain discipline among members, and employers can bust unions by subverting those disciplinary efforts.

Governments can counter wage suppression by providing legal protections for and subsidies to unions. This strategy has been pursued in many countries. In the United States, the law prohibits employers from engaging in various types of union-busting activities, including bribery of workers, intimidation, the creation of company unions, and much else. The law also regulates union elections, collective bargaining, and work stoppages. These regulations limit fraud and coercion, enhance transparency, and encourage peaceful negotiation and collective actions.

Unions operating in monopsonistic labor markets also generate spillovers to other, nonunion, workers. This is because union density raises wages for unionized employers, and nonunion employers must raise their wages to compete for workers.

Collective bargaining by unions may allow contracting to overcome a lack of competition. In an extreme example, where the marginal product of labor is constant, transferring monopoly power to workers can be efficient: rather than wages being distorted downward by monopsony, resulting in too few workers, the union will set the wage equal to marginal revenue product (having no reason to set it higher than that, as then the firm exits). In a more realistic case, the choice between laissez-faire monopsony and union monopoly will depend on a variety of factors. Evidence is mixed.[18]

Despite the legal protections they have been given, unions have lost ground in the United States over the past fifty years. There are many reasons for this, including technological change and globalization. Employers have developed more sophisticated union-busting strategies; workers have become increasingly isolated from each other as a result of broad economic trends, and this isolation interferes with organization; and right-to-work laws at the state level have further weakened union discipline by allowing workers to free-ride on the collective bargaining efforts of the union leadership.[19] Many employers have taken advantage of legal forms that allow them to classify workers as independent contractors (as discussed above) or fragment their workforce by operating through franchisees. General economic changes have also apparently created more highly differentiated jobs, which further interferes with organization as well as supplying employers with an independent source of market power.

8.9. Shareholder Activism/Codetermination

Monopsony implies that a component of firm profit is rents from underpriced labor. This profit then accrues to shareholders. But what if at least some of these shareholders are workers themselves?

Suppose workers own a portion of the firm's shares, and managers weight shareholders' interests according to shares held. Then the monopsony incentive to distort the wage downward is mitigated to the extent that the firm's manager internalizes the wage bill. Of course, if the labor supply is the extensive margin (number of workers), the question of how many workers a worker-owned firm would want needs to be answered, and that depends on how profits are shared and the extent of diminishing returns.[20]

A prominent example of employee ownership is employee stock ownership plans. Roughly 20% of private-sector American workers own some of the stock of their company. There is some evidence that employee ownership is linked to better company performance.[21] Part of the mechanism (besides higher compensation and effort and less conflict) is lower turnover and absenteeism. However, clearly identified causal effects of employee ownership are still missing from the literature.

Union pension funds have been used successfully to influence how employers treat workers. By organizing shareholders around worker interests and mobilizing proxy votes, union pension funds are able to influence a variety of firm decisions. But most pension funds, wanting diversification of risk, would likely invest only a small share of their savings in the firms that employ their members. And workers' holdings may be small relative to holdings of other investors.

By asking its managers to raise wages in monopsony, the pension fund would (a) lose some value in profits but (b) increase contributions and membership. Depending on the degree of monopsony, exposure to the firm, and the extent of contributions of workers, the value to the pension fund of (b) could offset the costs from (a).

Another example involves public-sector union pension funds, for example, CalPERS, which manages the pensions of California public employees. If one takes literally the idea that these funds should maximize the returns to their members, then it may sometimes be appropriate for these funds to demand that monopsonistic firms raise wages. Higher wages benefit the workers more than their lost capital gains. Tax revenues should also increase because the tax rate on wages is higher than the tax rate on capital gains—although the problem is complicated because the public goods funded by these tax gains will benefit people other than members, and the taxes paid on capital gains will mostly be paid by nonmembers as well. But to the extent that the tax bill increases, and to the extent that public-sector union members get higher wages from additional tax revenue, public-sector pension funds may have an interest in requiring their holdings to raise wages.

Codetermination, which is common in Germany, is often mentioned in this context. Rather than own shares of the firm, workers get votes on firm policies, including wage-setting policies. To the extent that workers' votes count, this will influence firm wage-setting and mitigate the exercise of monopsony power.

***

This survey of the impact of labor and employment law on employment and wages in conditions of monopsonistic competition only scratches the surface of a complex topic but it offers two lessons. First, many of these laws need to be rethought and reformed. One question is whether the laws should be narrowly tailored to market conditions. Minimum wage laws, for example, work better in monopsonistic markets than in (relatively) competitive markets, and this raises the question of whether they should be limited to monopsonistic labor markets. In principle, minimum wage laws should also be tailored so that the minimum wage varies from market to market, although this could introduce complexity and invite gaming by employers.

Second, labor market monopsony poses significantly greater challenges to policy than product market imperfections, where the relatively simple tradition of antitrust plus regulation of natural monopolies remains plausible—though it has come under increasing pressure in recent years as a result of the rise of Big Tech. People depend far more on work for their livelihoods and self-respect than they do on this or that good or service, and labor markets are shot through with frictions that all but guarantee wage suppression and a degree of unemployment. No clear formula has yet been invented for solving this problem, and for the foreseeable future it seems we may be able to do no more than tinker with modest technical reforms.

9

The Gig Economy and Independent Contractors

THE LAW RECOGNIZES A distinction between two types of worker: employees and independent contractors (or, merely, "contractors"). A person with the required skills—a plumber, electrician, nurse, accountant, lawyer, janitor—can work in either capacity. Yet the legal differences are significant. A worker classified as an employee is protected by the minimum wage law; a contractor is not. An employee can join a union, while a contractor who tried to organize a union would violate the antitrust laws. This chapter explains why this distinction is made and relates it to the problem of regulating labor monopsony.

Controversies relating to the distinction between employees and contractors have been much in the news. As a result of advances in technology, some workers who have traditionally been classified as employees are now being treated as contractors: they make a living by undertaking a series of "gigs" for different "labor buyers" (as I will call the firms or households that purchase the services of workers) rather than working for a single employer.[1] Many commentators worry that these gig contractors are being exploited because they are not entitled to the protections of employment law;[2] a related view is that workers who are really employees are being deliberately misclassified as contractors by rapacious employers for the same reason.[3]

While new technology and employment trends have highlighted these problems, the problems themselves are not new. The distinction between employees and contractors is deeply entrenched in the law and reflects a basic intuition about the organization of labor markets. Consider, for example, a person trained as an electrician. She might choose to set up her own business. She advertises her services and spends her days working for various homeowners who pay her to repair the fuse box or install new lighting. The electrician seems like a business owner, not an employee, and indeed she would be legally classified as an independent contractor. Or she might go to work for, say, a company that needs someone to repair fuse boxes and install lighting in its warehouses. She shows up at a worksite every day at 9 a.m., leaves at 5 p.m., and draws a salary from a single firm. She takes orders from a boss rather than performing tasks for a customer. Here, she would be classified as an employee. And as an employee, she would be protected by numerous federal and state laws that control wages, working conditions, and benefits. If instead she works as a contractor, she would enjoy none of these legal protections.

Because the same person doing the same type of work might be self-employed or an employee of someone else, the distinction between employee and contractor can be elusive. The distinction is made more complicated still by the administrative requirements that have grown up around it. Because contractors often charge for a job rather than by the hour, it may be difficult to calculate an hourly wage, and thus to apply the minimum wage laws to them. Because contractors often work alone, it might seem that the right to organize a union would do them no good. Because contractors often choose their own tools and control working conditions, it would make little sense to compel those who buy their labor to comply with legal requirements for workplace safety. Contractors often work for homeowners and other consumers who lack the legal sophistication and administrative resources for complying with the huge number of legal restrictions that apply to employers, including the obligation to withhold taxes. And, until recently, it was common to think of contractors as highly trained professionals—electricians, plumbers, lawyers, doctors—who were not as vulnerable to mistreatment by buyers of their labor as ordinary employees were. Contractors did not seem to need employment law protections.

But technology has put pressure on these intuitions. Companies can now organize their businesses so that drivers, janitors, and home healthcare workers are classified as contractors rather than employees. Compensation can be structured so that it is hourly or based on the accomplishment of tasks; control over working conditions can be assigned to the worker, retained by an organization, or divided between them; and organizations can match workers with consumers so that consumers, rather than the organization, seem like the employers. Organizations can knit workers together into loose teams, keep them apart from each other, or use them as a conventional workforce; they can assign the price-setting power to workers or keep it for themselves. Or both: Uber normally sets wages for drivers but recently has allowed drivers in some cities to set their own prices up to five times a base price.[4] With the scrambling of categories, the intuitions have lost their force, and it is necessary to look deeper for the policy reasons behind the distinction between employee and contractor.

9.1. Discrete and Relational Work

At least as far back as Ronald Coase's paper "The Nature of the Firm," published in 1937, economists have identified the distinguishing feature of employment as the employer's control over the worker.[5] An employee is "in" the firm because the managers of the firm can issue orders to her and expect her obedience. A contractor is "outside" the firm because the managers of the firm can elicit cooperation only through a negotiated bargain. The idea of control has also been central to the common-law definition of employment (or master-servant) relationships for centuries.[6] But the nature of control has turned out to be elusive. Criticizing Coase's reliance on control for the definition of the employment relationship, economists Armen Alchian and Harold Demsetz pointed out that a customer exerts control over a contractor as well.[7] For example, if a grocer refuses to do what a customer wants—stock a certain product, for example—the customer may stop patronizing the business. The fear of losing customers puts the grocer under customers' control—just as the stock clerk's fear of being fired causes her to obey the grocery store owner's order to fill the shelves with one product rather than another.

A moment's reflection, however, reveals the problem with this argument. Suppose a customer tells a grocer to move the candy bars to a shelf where children will not see them, or to sweep the floor because it is too dirty, or to change the window display. Even at risk of losing the customer, the grocer is likely to tell him to get lost. By contrast, a grocer could certainly tell her stock clerks to do any of these things. While the stock clerks could refuse and quit, most likely they would obey the grocer's directions. The control that an employer exerts over an employee is different from the kind of control that a customer exerts over a contractor.

A line of literature has made progress with the notion of control, rooting it in the idea that contracts—including employment contracts—can never fully specify the optimal actions of the parties, and so unavoidably allocate discretion among them.[8] As a rough approximation, contracts between labor buyers and workers that allocate key aspects of discretion to the labor buyers create employment relationships, while those that allocate those aspects of discretion to the workers create contract relationships. In the balance of this section and the next, I draw on this literature. Then I will turn to its implications for the misclassification test.

To understand what "control" means in the employment context, consider a simple example. A person I will call the Rider needs a car and driver in order to get around town. The Rider may choose between two arrangements. Under the first, the Rider owns a car and contracts with a person, the Driver, to chauffer her for a period of time. Under the second, the Rider does not own the car; the Driver does. The Rider and the Driver enter a contract under which the Driver agrees to drive the Rider around for a period of time.

The two contracts look nearly identical, and it is easy to imagine that in practice the "output"—the routes used by the Driver, the amenities of the service, and so on—is identical under both contracts. If the Driver is capital-constrained, the Rider could lend him the money to buy the car, and now the two contracts seem even more similar. We can further imagine that the parties, in each case, enter into highly detailed contracts that specify numerous attributes of the relationship: when the Driver must show up every day, how far the Driver must drive, even the routes and any chitchat that will take place while the Driver and Rider share the car.

Yet there is an important difference. When the Rider owns the car, the Rider enjoys "residual control," meaning control over how the car is used where the contract fails to specify the Driver's obligations. And when the Driver owns the car, the Driver enjoys residual control. As a concrete example, imagine that the parties enter into a 100-page contract that specifies nearly every aspect of the work relationship but omits, say, whether the Driver can talk on the phone with friends while driving the Rider. If the Driver does talk on the phone, and the Rider objects, the assignment of residual control matters. If the Driver owns the car, and the Rider tells him to stop talking to his friends, he can simply refuse because he is not prohibited from doing so under the contract. If the Rider fires him, she breaches the contract. She could offer to pay him more to stop talking to his friends, and he may agree, but this additional bargain is costly to negotiate, and the Driver has the bargaining power. If the Rider does not have good alternative people to hire as the Driver (and is reluctant to approach a stranger who has not acquired what we will call relationship-specific knowledge), the Driver can "hold up" the Rider for a high additional price.

If the Rider owns the car and tells the driver to stop talking to his friends, the Driver is required to obey. He does not have residual control over the car and cannot use it in ways prohibited by the owner. Of course, the Driver could quit. But now the Rider has the bargaining power. The Driver might prefer to work and might be willing to accept a reduction in wages in return for the right to speak, but now he has to pay the Rider for this right. If the Driver has made a relationship-specific investment—preferring to drive *this* Rider rather than other people because he has learned her needs and doesn't want to have to learn the needs and idiosyncrasies of a new boss—he will need to make concessions.

The parties will assign the property interest (that is, car ownership) to the party whose use of residual control is more likely to maximize the surplus of their interaction. Consider first the Driver. If the Driver owns the car, then he will be given strong incentives to maintain the car. He will drive it carefully and take it to the garage frequently. He will anticipate that in the future the relationship may end, and he will want the car in good working order as he searches for new customers. I will call this behavior "worker care."

The problem with maximizing worker care is that the worker may have correspondingly weak incentives to follow the Rider's orders. The

Rider might order the Driver to take the fastest route, and the Driver might prefer not to because the fastest route is a potholed road that is hard on the car. The Driver might therefore choose another route. The Rider might be willing to tolerate a car that is less than perfectly maintained in return for greater obedience. I call the Rider's concern "worker coordination," by which I mean the value of coordination between the worker's action and assets owned by, or other workers managed by, the labor buyer, here the Rider. To ensure worker coordination, the Rider requires "managerial direction" (or "managerial discretion," to emphasize the freedom to direct the Driver); specification of optimal Driver behavior by contract is impossible.

Thus, when the parties negotiate the contract, they will trade off these two values. If car maintenance is more important than control over the route (say, because the city is laid out in a grid and there are few routes to choose), then the parties will assign ownership to the Driver. The Driver will take care of the car to maintain its value. But car maintenance may not be a serious issue because the car is well constructed, and poor maintenance will not significantly reduce its value. In that case, the parties will assign the car to the Rider, who will enjoy greater control over the Driver. In this economic sense, the Driver is a contractor in the first case, and an employee in the second.

A useful real-world example comes from a paper by economists George Baker and Thomas Hubbard, which examines the shift from the owner-operator model of trucking to the company driver model.[9] Owner-operators are independent contractors; they own their trucks and contract with shippers. Company drivers are employees; they work for a single, usually very large shipper. For truckers, "worker care" is the same as in my example of the Driver-Rider relationship: "Wear and tear on the truck is minimized when drivers drive at a steady and moderate speed, but drivers may prefer to drive fast and then take long breaks because it allows them to rest longer, visit friends, etc., and still arrive on time."[10] Worker coordination is also important because "hauls vary in their desirability to drivers in ways that are not captured in agreements with carriers. Those that take drivers into congested or dangerous areas are less desirable," as do those that take drivers to remote areas where there are no desirable "backhauls," that is, return trips with a new load of cargo.[11] The problem faced by the shipper and the trucker is how to optimize care (minimizing wear and tear) while ensuring that the best routes are taken.

When drivers operate as contractors, they have strong worker care incentives: they drive their truck carefully because they own it. But they are reluctant to take less desirable routes, and thus dispatchers—who coordinate routes—must negotiate with them case by case, which is disruptive. When drivers operate as company drivers, they have weak worker care incentives because the company bears the mainte-nance cost. But the company can simply order drivers to take the route that is optimal for the company. Here, we see the basic trade-off in action. Baker and Hubbard hypothesize that longer hauls create greater problems for worker effort because there are more opportunities for the driver to engage in the suboptimal speed-and-rest strategy, while the backhaul negotiation problem seems the same for long-haul and short-haul drivers. The hypothesis finds support in evidence showing that long-haul drivers are more likely to be owner-operators than short-haul drivers are. The authors also examine the effect of the introduc-tion of on-board computers, which monitor driver performance and thus reduce the worker's ability to shirk on worker care. The evidence indicates, as one would expect, that the introduction of this monitoring technology substantially reduced the share of owner-operated (con-tractor) trucks.[12]

To sum up, a labor buyer and a worker maximize their joint surplus by assigning the relevant property right to the worker when care is more important than other actions that require management direction and coordination. The worker owns the asset and is called a contractor. Otherwise, the labor buyer owns the asset and the worker is called an employee. The contract that governs their relationship will help ensure that the asset is used, as much as possible, to the parties' joint benefit. If the worker owns the car, the contract will provide that the employer directs the worker. If the employer owns the car, the contract will pro-vide that the worker take care of the car. The relative extent to which these obligations can be written into the contract will determine which relationship is chosen.

A major difference between an employee (who interacts with assets owned by the firm as well as the firm's other workers) and a contractor (who interacts with assets owned by the contractor herself) is that the employee makes a relationship-specific investment in the "firm," which is to say in the assets owned by the firm and the other employees of the firm. The contractor does not make a relationship-specific investment, or much more limited investment. This difference is related to two concepts I discussed earlier: contract specificity and worker coordination.

When a contract can be specified in a relatively substantial sense, the underlying reason is that the task in question is standardized— routine, predictable, the same in different contexts. For example, when a homeowner hires a locksmith to fix a lock, the task is fully specified by the customer (though usually on the basis of a custom that the contract references rather than through detailed contractual specification). The locksmith performs the same task from place to place and does not need to learn anything about the individual interests or needs of different homeowners. Many tasks cannot be specified, however. An elderly homeowner who hires a personal companion to keep her company, maintain her records, deal with outsiders, and so on, will expect the companion to invest a great deal of time and effort in learning the homeowner's needs, interests, and ways of doing things. As a result, the companion's work is "relational," in the sense that abilities the companion obtains over time as a result of frequent interaction with the homeowner are not easily transferable to other contexts—so if the companion quits and goes to work for someone else, she will start again from the beginning with a new employer.

Thus, I distinguish between "discrete work" like the locksmith's and "relational work" like the companion's. The homeowner's concern is "worker coordination," the need to ensure that the companion will do just what the homeowner requires. The homeowner does not need, or needs less, worker coordination with respect to the locksmith, who relies on his own, transferable training and experience when he fixes the lock. The locksmith is a contractor; the companion is an employee.

The nature of work—relational or discrete—does not necessarily depend on the profession. A locksmith might be a contractor or an employee in different contexts. Let us consider a more complex example involving two lawyers. Andrew is a solo practitioner who drafts wills for clients. He operates out of an office that he rents from a commercial landlord. Most of Andrew's clients see him only once or a small number of times over their lives. He has drafted wills for thousands of people. It takes him only an hour or so to draft a will in most cases.

Beth is a tax attorney who works full time in the family office of a noted tycoon. She works 9 to 5 in a suite of offices with several other workers—accountants, investment advisers, and other lawyers. She works closely with this team and consults frequently with the tycoon and various family members. She does not work outside the office; like most other workers in this office, she has worked there for many years and is vague about when or even whether she might leave for a different job.

Andrew and Beth attended the same law school and received the same legal training, but their skills are by now quite different. Andrew's body of knowledge—a deep understanding of testamentary law and related areas of law—allows him to offer identical services to numerous people. His skill (or human capital) is general.[13] Moreover, while his clients all have different financial resources and needs, along the relative dimension for which they hire Andrew—the disposition of their assets at death—the services that he offers are very similar, one might even say commodified. We can thus think of Andrew's work as *discrete* in the following sense: the value of the service he offers is independent of his relationship with the client—whether he has known the client for a long time, for example. Andrew's work is discrete in another sense: its value to the client is independent of Andrew's relationship with other workers. He works alone. The nature of his skills—his knowledge of testamentary law, plus his ability to listen to and understand his clients—enables him to offer discrete services to a range of clients.

Beth, like Andrew, possesses a body of knowledge that she brings to bear as she provides services for her client, the tycoon. When she first goes to work for the family office, she brings the same type of discrete skill to the operations of the office as Andrew would. But after working for a few years for the client, the nature of the skill has changed significantly. The hiring launches a relationship, and it is in the context of this relationship that most of Beth's value is generated. Over time, she develops an increasingly deep understanding of the client's resources, needs, and idiosyncrasies. She also develops an understanding of the other workers: how they work together, what they need from her, the appropriate way to behave in the office, and so on. Unlike Andrew, Beth engages in primarily relational work in the following sense: the value of the service she offers is dependent on her relationship with the client and with her coworkers (and specific assets owned by the employer, for example, office equipment or, more plausibly, bespoke software and records). As a rough approximation, the longer and deeper the relationship, the greater the value that Beth confers on the family office. Beth's major skills are thus relationship-specific. Aside from her knowledge of the law, the skills she develops at the family office—including her skills in working with others—generate value.

We can now return to the concepts of contract specificity and managerial direction. Because Andrew's work produces a relatively standard product, the customers do not need control, that is, managerial direction, over how Andrew does his work. The customer merely supplies some information in advance that Andrew uses to conform the product at the margin to the customer's needs. In contrast, because Beth's product is constantly changing in response to changing conditions and the idiosyncratic needs of the firm she works for, someone—the manager or the person who coordinates the joint production of all the workers in the family office—is given managerial direction over Beth's work.

The distinction between discrete and relational work is an old one. In the Middle Ages, craft workers typically proceeded through two stages: a relational and a discrete stage.[14] The relational stage was the apprenticeship, during which the worker worked for a single master and became steadily more valuable to the master as he gained experience both at the craft and at serving the master's interests. Once the apprenticeship was over, the worker could sell his services, now discrete work, to the market, by forging swords, cobbling shoes, or building walls—directly for customers. During the Industrial Revolution, some workers worked in teams at factories, while others did piecework at home. The factory workers did relational work and today would be regarded as employees. The pieceworkers did discrete work, often at home, and resembled contractors. There have been cases in which a single worksite housed workers who worked in teams and workers who worked independently on components; the latter group of workers thought of themselves as craftsmen with higher status than the first group of workers, who resembled today's employees.[15] In the pre-internet age of the twentieth century, relational work continued in factories and other workplaces, while discrete work was often conducted by skilled professionals—plumbers, doctors, artists, writers, lawyers. Thus, the notion that some work lends itself to relationships and other work does not is not a new one; it is a thread that runs through the history of labor relations.

9.2. Market Structure

The distinction between relational and discrete work matters for policy because it roughly maps onto a distinction in market structure.[16] Because the seller of discrete work maximizes the value of the work without entering into relationships with buyers, she can sell that work to many different buyers. The "cost of exit"—the cost to the worker if any specific labor buyer stops buying from her—is low because the worker can simply find another labor buyer. (Think of the locksmith who goes from household to household and will not be significantly harmed if one household stops using her services.) The market for discrete work is thus (relatively) competitive. By contrast, the seller of relational work maximizes the value of that work by working for a single labor buyer and remaining with that buyer for an extended period of time. She must make a relationship-specific investment in assets owned by the labor buyer and in other people who work for the labor buyer. This means that the highest-value buyer of the worker's labor is the person or firm for whom the worker already works, and thus that the worker's cost of exit is high. The market is (relatively) monopsonistic.

By definition, a relational worker who works for an employer is subject to monopsony pressure. Because her services are worth more to the current employer than (in normal cases) to another employer, the current employer can pay her more than any outside employer. But by the same token the worker's outside options are limited. If she earns $100,000 at the current employer, and outside employers will offer only $50,000, then she cannot make a credible threat to leave if the current employer stops giving her raises. The current employer has strong incentives to limit wage increases (or even to reduce wages) or to worsen working conditions (for example, by demanding more work after hours). As labor economists have observed, virtually all employers thus have monopsony power. The usual explanation is that search costs and job differentiation give rise to frictions, but the simpler way of putting this is that work for employers is relational. The buyer of discrete work, by contrast, has no such power.

A possible objection to this argument is that people who apply to become relational workers can protect themselves by demanding an employment contract that protects them from such ex post exploitation. When Beth applies for the position with the family office, she is effectively a discrete worker (with a commodified body of knowledge about tax law) who hopes to obtain relationship-specific skills and the higher compensation that comes with them. If she is rational and far-sighted, however, she knows that as she develops these skills, the family office will be able to use its market power over her to pay her less than her marginal revenue product. To protect herself, she could, in principle, demand that her compensation rise indefinitely as her marginal revenue product rises, and insist on a contract to that effect. If the family office breaches, she would be able to sue for damages.

This counterargument brings us back to the issue of contract specificity. The property rights literature on which I draw takes for granted the impossibility of such contracting; that is why residual control is so important. Because the parties cannot specify value-maximizing behavior in advance, they assign residual control to whichever party has the best incentives to use it to generate a surplus. Empirically, such bargaining is rarely observed, most likely because the employer does not trust a court to determine the marginal revenue product of a particular employee and requires flexibility to adjust wages and working conditions in response to external shocks. It may also be that few employees have the sophistication to demand such contracts—perhaps aside from a handful of highly experienced, highly skilled employees who can hire agents and lawyers to protect them. And if few job applicants are sophisticated and wealthy enough to bargain for wage protection, then employers do better by looking for those who lack sophistication. Thus, the competition for workers that takes place when a soon-to-be-relational worker is hired (say, recent law school graduates) does not translate into market protection for those workers years or decades later in their careers.

As a general proposition, discrete workers are protected by competition for their work; relational workers are not. By "protected," I mean merely that the workers are paid the efficient wage, their marginal revenue product—the wage necessary to maximize production—rather than a lower wage.

The argument is a generalization; exceptions exist. While relational work unavoidably generates monopsony, markets for discrete work are not always competitive. I will return to this issue below.

I have argued that work can be divided into discrete and relational types and that discrete work tends to yield competitive labor markets while relational work tends to yield monopsonized labor markets. Why does this matter? The answer is that the appropriate legal protections are different for workers in monopsonized labor markets and workers in competitive labor markets. Where markets are monopsonized, they fail: they produce inefficiently low output. Legal regulation is called for, and it takes the form of what is conventionally called "employment law" and "labor law." The label of the first body of law should come as no surprise given my claim that workers who face monopsonized conditions are properly called "employees." Where markets are competitive, they do not fail. Legal regulation is not called for—at least not required for the purpose of correcting a market failure.[17] This is why there is no separate body of "contractor" law that confers protections on contractors. Table 9.1 summarizes the argument to this point.

This is why classification matters. When workers engage in discrete work in competitive labor markets, they should be classified as contractors because competition adequately protects them, while employment and labor law can do little good for them and possibly cause harm to them and society at large. When workers engage in relational work in uncompetitive labor markets, they should be classified as employees because both employment and labor law can help them, and in a socially beneficial way.

Employment law and labor law reflect different approaches to labor relations, and so I will discuss them separately. Among economists, employment law protections have always been a bit of a puzzle. In a perfectly competitive labor market, employment laws cannot benefit workers and will likely harm them.[18] Consider the minimum wage. If the labor market is competitive and the market wage exceeds the minimum wage, the minimum wage law does not affect wages. If the market wage is below the minimum wage, then employers will fire

TABLE 9.1. The Contractor/Employee Distinction

Legal Label	Labor Market	Type of Work	Property Right	Investment	Important Incentive	Exit Cost	Regulation
Contractor	Competitive	Discrete	Worker	General	Worker care	Low	None
Employee	Monopsonized	Relational	Labor buyer	Relationship-specific	Worker coordination	High	Employment and labor law

workers who generate benefits less than their wage cost. While the wage of other workers may rise, in aggregate workers will be harmed.

Labor law is also a puzzle from this standpoint, although for a different reason. Labor law authorizes workers to organize a union even though the agreement among workers in a union to strike if they are not paid the same wage, or according to the same compensation schedule, is equivalent to a price- (or actually wage-) fixing cartel. If the labor market is competitive, then the employer would be required to pay market wages to the workers. If the workers cartelize the labor market through the union, they can insist on an above-market wage, which would reduce both overall employment in the labor market and output, which would probably raise prices for consumers as well. If labor markets are competitive, there would be no reason for the government to encourage or even tolerate unions.

However, as we have seen, labor markets are not competitive. Search costs and related frictions ensure that employers enjoy labor monopsony; labor market concentration, which exists in most employment markets, further enhances employers' market power.[19] In conditions of labor monopsony, employment law and labor law have stronger justifications.

The best illustration of this claim is the debate about minimum wage laws, which have been subject to extensive empirical research. The traditional view of economists assumed competitive labor markets and held that minimum wage laws cannot benefit workers and can only harm them. Yet after years of controversy, there is increasing evidence that minimum wage laws have not had this predicted disemployment effect: they have usually raised wage levels without reducing employment.[20] While this result contradicts the assumption of competitive labor markets, it is compatible with labor monopsony. Monopsonistic employers do not fire workers after a compelled wage increase because a monopsonist will make money off workers even when forced to pay above the monopsony wage as long as the minimum wage is not too high. The minimum wage law pushes wages toward the competitive rate that would prevail in a competitive market. And if the minimum wage is closer to the competitive wage than the monopsony wage is, the minimum wage will result in higher employment—since more workers will work for the higher wage.[21]

Similarly, labor law is a straightforward legal response to the problem of monopsonized labor markets. If the employer enjoys a monopsony over workers, then it can pay a wage lower than the marginal revenue product. The main reason that employers can do this is that workers rarely have a credible threat to quit if they are paid below the market wage—again because of search costs, employer concentration, and related frictions. Workers can increase their market power by agreeing among themselves to quit en masse (that is, strike) if the employer refuses to pay them a higher wage. As a result, the wage should be pushed toward the competitive level (though unions could demand wages higher than the competitive level if they are powerful enough). Labor law could be justified for its role in preventing employers from using aggressive tactics to defeat organizations so as to preserve their market power over wages.

We can now see why the law goes to such trouble to classify workers as "contractors" and "employees" and why employers try so hard to reclassify employees as contractors. Employees benefit from legal protection because they are subject to labor monopsony and hence are not protected by market competition. Employment law protections prevent employers from using their monopsony power to push down wages and worsen conditions. Labor law enables workers to counter employer monopsony power with their own aggregated bargaining power. Contractors do not benefit from employment law protections because market competition already protects them, while the right to organize would enable them to form cartels that charge above-market prices.[22] The market protects contractors because their discrete skills are valued similarly by numerous labor buyers. And this is why firms that buy work from relational workers have an incentive to misclassify them as contractors; by doing so, they evade employment and labor laws that restrict their ability to exercise monopsony power over their workers.

It is important to see that this justification for employment and labor law—for limiting the law to employees rather than extending it to contractors—is based on market structure, not on income inequality or poverty, which is the focus of much academic work. From an empirical standpoint, the market structure theory is clearly superior. Employment and labor law protects wealthy employees as well as poor employees; contractors are deprived of that protection regardless of whether they are rich or poor. From a normative standpoint, the market structure theory is superior as well. Employment law and labor law counter labor monopsony, which should generate wealth. While employment and labor law under this understanding should also redistribute wealth from on-average wealthier investors to on-average poorer employers, it does not do so in a targeted way.[23] The bodies of law also do nothing for the very poor, who are often out of work. Traditional antipoverty programs and tax-and-transfers are a more suitable way to address the problems of poverty and inequality.

9.3. Misclassification

Because employment and labor law restricts firms' ability to exploit their labor monopsony power, firms have an incentive to classify workers as contractors, regardless of whether the workers are employees in an economic sense, that is, workers who are subject to managerial direction and face a high cost of exit because of their relationship-specific investments in the firm. Uber's classification of drivers as contractors has attracted public attention, but the problem is a long-standing one.

Courts use various tests to resolve disputes over whether a worker is an employee or an independent contractor. The common-law test turned on "control": the worker is an employee if the labor buyer "controls" her, and an independent contractor otherwise.[24] While that test was originally developed to determine whether a labor buyer is liable for torts committed by a worker, it continues to be used for classification issues in the employment context.[25] For federal legislation that protects the rights of workers, the relevant test is the "economic reality" or "economic dependence" test: a worker is an employee if she is "dependent" on the labor buyer.[26] Related state legislation uses similar tests.

The economic dependence test involves six factors:

1. the nature and degree of the alleged employer's control as to the manner in which the work is to be performed;
2. the alleged employee's opportunity for profit or loss depending upon his managerial skill;

3. the alleged employee's investment in equipment or materials required for his task, or his employment of workers;
4. whether the service rendered requires a special skill;
5. the degree of permanency and duration of the working relationship;
6. the extent to which the service rendered is an integral part of the alleged employer's business.[27]

Commentators agree that courts apply this test inconsistently.[28] Part of the problem is that all these factors are vague, and relationships between labor buyers and workers are extremely diverse. It is easy to think of examples of employees who have a great deal of control over their work (traveling salesmen); who are paid bonuses based on managerial skill (managers, for example); who have special skills (industrial scientist); and so on. But the main problem is that the normative goal of the test has been forgotten or perhaps was never fully understood, and so there is no single principle that disciplines how courts apply the various factors.

The solution is a test grounded in the normative goal of employment and labor law, which, as I have argued, is to counter labor monopsony where workers make relationship-specific investments and face high exit costs. The two major factors—economic dependence and control—are unified: a worker is economically dependent on an employer because of the high costs of exit, and because of the high cost of exit the worker is willing to subject herself to the firm's control. Thus, economic dependence does not mean poverty; it means labor monopsony. Economic dependence and control are not in tension; they are different aspects of the employment relationship.

According to the "relational work" test, as I will call it, a worker is a person who performs activities ("work") for another person in return for pay. A worker is an employee of a firm (or household) when the worker's cost of finding alternative work of the same type and at the same level of pay is high ("high exit option"). A worker has a high exit option when the work is "relational"; that is, the work is worth more if performed for a single firm over time than if performed in discrete units. In short: employment is relational work; independent contractor status arises for discrete work.

Seen in this way, the factors used in the economic dependence test can be given greater specificity:

1. Control. When work is relational, the labor buyer retains "control" over the worker, in the sense of discretionary authority over the worker's behavior as the worker performs services. Control in this sense is necessary because the labor buyer must constantly coordinate the worker's work with the work of others. In contrast, discrete work can be largely specified by contract in advance of the work; thus, the labor buyer does not retain control, that is, discretionary authority, over the worker's behavior as the worker performs tasks.

2. Opportunity for profit or loss depending upon the workers' managerial skill. When work is relational, the worker allows herself to be managed by the labor buyer, who directly, or through subordinates, coordinates the behavior of multiple workers or adjusts work in response to the buyer's changing needs. The independent contractor uses managerial skill in the course of contracting herself out to multiple labor buyers, and thus is compensated for that managerial skill as well as taking on the risk of managerial failure that results in the loss of clients and hence profits.

3. Investment in equipment or materials required for a task, or employment of workers. This factor reflects the importance of the assignment of property rights so as to locate discretion in the party that is most likely to use it to maximize the surplus. When the work is discrete, the property right is assigned to the worker. When the worker is relational, the property right is assigned to the employer.

4. The service rendered requires a special skill. If we interpret "special" to mean relational, this factor fits the relational test. A plumber's skill is the same whether the plumber is self-employed or employed by a firm; what is special about the skill in the second case is that the plumber adjusts it, through relationship-specific investment, so it satisfies the unique needs of that employer.

5. The degree of permanency and duration of the working relationship. Because the value of relational work is highest for

the labor buyer with whom the worker has a relationship, and low for other potential labor buyers, the relational worker will tend to remain with the labor buyer in question. Discrete workers, by contrast, may move from labor buyer to labor buyer.

6. The extent to which the service rendered is an integral part of the labor buyer's business. Relational work, unlike discrete work, is integral, in the sense that it is valuable to the extent that it is used in the operations of the labor buyer with whom the worker has a relationship.

This gloss of the factors in the economic dependence test shows that they can be integrated into the relational work framework. My claim is not, however, that the courts consistently interpret the factors in this way. On the contrary, in the hands of the courts, the factors have become unmoored from any plausible goal of employment and labor legislation. The courts frequently seem more focused on whether workers are low-income than on whether they are economically dependent in the market-structure sense. But, as noted earlier, low-income status is not a reason for classifying workers as employees rather than as independent contractors.

In 2019, the California state legislature passed a law that expanded and simplified its definition of "employee." The earlier test resembled the federal economic dependence test. The new law provided that anyone who works for remuneration is an employee unless the labor buyer shows that:

A. The person is free from the control and direction of the hiring entity in connection with the performance of the work, both under the contract for the performance of the work and in fact.
B. The person performs work that is outside the usual course of the hiring entity's business.
C. The person is customarily engaged in an independently established trade, occupation, or business of the same nature as that involved in the work performed.[29]

The first provision repeats the control test, and the third provision reflects the idea that discrete work can, and often will, be performed independently of a single labor buyer. But the second provision is broader than the federal rule. It also seems questionable. Under the second provision, a plumbing "contractor" who establishes contacts with plumbers and contracts them out to households would be deemed an employer rather than a contractor. This is hard to justify under the relational work test. This matchmaker function is not relational: the individual plumbers who are contracted out would not normally need to invest in assets owned by the "contractor." A computer dating service does not "employ" its customers but sells a service to them. The mere fact that a plumber rather than someone other than a plumber (say, a "general contractor") matches plumber to project should not convert a contractor relationship to an employment relationship.

9.4. The Misclassification Debate

Gig-economy workers float somewhere between the traditional employee and the traditional contractor. Take the case of Uber. Drivers control some aspects of their work (they choose their automobile, within constraints; they choose when to work) and not others (choice of routes); they do not manage anyone, but they do invest in equipment, including the automobile itself; they do not seem to exercise a special skill (driving), but they are free to switch among other labor buyers, including other ride-sharing companies and their own clients. Drivers sometimes seem economically dependent in the traditional sense because most of them earn a paltry sum for their work, but they are not economically dependent in the sense of being dependent on just one company, or even on the occupation of driving. Other gig-economy firms locate their workers in other places along the spectrum from contractor to employee. Some workers are allowed to negotiate with customers, set their prices, and exert greater control over working conditions, while others are given less control and are prohibited from using other platforms. Critics argue that firms evade the spirit of the employment laws by giving workers minimal freedoms or responsibilities necessary to qualify them for contractor status rather than allowing those conditions to be determined by the nature of the business.

The controversy over Uber's classification of drivers as contractors provides a good illustration. Drivers use "effort" to drive expeditiously and maintain their cars. By allocating ownership of the cars to the drivers, Uber gives them high-powered incentives to maintain their cars. But it is easy to imagine the alternative approach in which Uber owns the cars. While the drivers' care incentives would be diminished, Uber would gain greater control over other aspects of their work— for example, the level of courtesy they offer passengers, which may be important for Uber's brand. If Uber owns the cars, then its threat to punish discourteous drivers is strengthened: it can not only kick the drivers off the platform (where drivers can use other platforms); it can take away their cars as well. The analysis is similar to the analysis of trucking, where (in my example) the courtesy problem takes the place of the backhaul problem in trucking.

From a legal perspective, the question is whether Uber classifies its drivers as contractors because it is important for workers to take care of their cars, and so it is important for workers to own them. If car maintenance contributes more economic value to ridesharing than courtesy does, then the classification of drivers as workers is correct. The drivers do not make relationship-specific investments in Uber's platform, and so the drivers are protected by competition—they can find work with other platforms or independently find clients—and so do not need the protection of the law.

Unfortunately, it is difficult to determine what Uber (or any other ridesharing or taxi or limousine company) would do in the absence of a legal regime that would push them to classify workers as contractors in order to avoid the costs of complying with employment and labor laws. A court or regulator can at best do a rough analysis. Applying the relational work test, the most striking aspect of the Uber case is that it (like the trucking companies after the introduction of on-board monitoring) imposes a considerable level of control over drivers through contract specificity (thanks to the platform technology). The platform allows Uber to control their level of courtesy with the star rating system, for example. And the platform allows Uber to assign the property right over the car to the worker so as to enhance the worker's motivation to take care. On the other hand, the monitoring technology that enables Uber to control the routes, courtesy, and other elements of the service would also enable it to monitor the driver's care level (as the trucking example shows). And the empirical evidence suggests that drivers cannot easily abandon the Uber platform once they begin using it,[30] suggesting a nontrivial relationship-specific investment in using and mastering the technology.

While I will not try to resolve the Uber question here, the example illustrates how the relational work test should be applied.

9.5. Misclassification and Antitrust

The gig economy has spawned antitrust suits that allege that firms like Uber have cartelized labor markets. However, while many commentators allege that Uber has exploited drivers, at least one group of plaintiffs argue that Uber coordinated price-fixing by drivers.[31] Which is it? Are drivers complicit wrongdoers or passive victims?

The problem comes back to the question of whether drivers are employees or contractors. Labor law assumes that employees lack bargaining power—that is, they face an employer-monopsonist—and gives them the right to organize so that they can counter the employer's bargaining power with their own. Antitrust law, for this reason, recognizes a labor exemption: employees do not violate antitrust law by organizing even though a union is a type of price- (or actually wage-) fixing arrangement.[32] Labor union organization when employees are subject to monopsony should increase production and (in many cases) lower prices, while raising wages as well. However, because contractors are not employees they do not benefit from the labor exemption and they are not permitted to organize.[33] Organization by contractors in a competitive market would result in a cartel, and hence less production and higher prices. That is why drivers who organize violate the law if they are contractors but not if they are employees.

The discussion should make clear how employment law protections mesh with antitrust and labor law to create a general legal structure that governs the relationships between workers and labor buyers. Antitrust law prohibits workers in competitive labor markets from forming cartels, while labor and employment law protects workers in monopsonized labor markets—labor law, by allowing them to organize, and employment law (including the minimum wage law), by regulating prices and conditions. On this view, workers are divided into "employees" who are subject to monopsony and "contractors" who are not.

Thus, it is important in the antitrust context to get straight the reasons why workers should be classified as employees or contractors. When workers operate in a competitive labor market, they should be classified as contractors, and thus forbidden to organize because the right to organize would result in cartelization and above-market wages/prices. When workers operate in a monopsonized labor market, they should be classified as employees, and thus allowed to organize because the right to organize should allow them to counter employer market power and thus raise wages toward the competitive level.

There are notable analogies on the product market side. When firms have natural monopolies, they are generally immune to antitrust challenge, but they may be subject to price regulation and related regulations designed to prevent them from abusing their market power. Given the parallel nature of product and labor markets, it should not be surprising that there are analogous rules on the labor side even if they have rarely been recognized as such because of the different legal terminology.

It is possible to argue that if employment and labor law counter labor monopsony power, the antitrust laws are not needed, and workers should not be permitted to bring antitrust actions against employers. But the two approaches to monopsony are complements. On the product market side, antitrust law coexists with various forms of price regulation, like usury laws, anti-price-gouging laws, and insurance premium limits. Antitrust law focuses on tactics employed by firms to increase their market power or extend monopolies into new markets, while price regulation limits the negative effects of firms that have achieved market power lawfully. Similarly, while antitrust law can be used to prevent firms from increasing their power over labor markets through collusion, mergers, and the like, other areas of law are needed to counter the negative effects of labor market power that is achieved lawfully.

A final point is that while I have assumed that discrete-work markets are competitive, they may not be. Discrete-work markets should be more competitive than relational-work markets because the discrete worker does not make a relationship-specific investment in a primary labor buyer and hence does not have high exit costs derived from the relationship. But a discrete worker may still face high exit costs if there are few labor buyers. Concentration arises simply because there are few buyers, and concentration could occur either legally (because there are economies of scale, for example) or illegally (because mergers result in a single dominant labor buyer). In this case, the logical source of legal protection for the discrete worker is antitrust law, which distinguishes between concentration that is regarded as socially harmful and concentration that is regarded as tolerable.

Conclusion: Whither Work?

ANTITRUST LAW NEGLECTS LABOR monopsony, and it shouldn't. The explanation for this state of affairs is not simple. Many factors play a role: the state of economic wisdom until recently, analysts' crude understanding of labor markets that has only recently been improved, the incentives of class action lawyers, among other things. As economic understanding of labor monopsony advances, the law needs to catch up.

Courts and regulators should crack down on employers. They must go beyond the most overt forms of collusion, like no-poaching agreements, and punish the more subtle forms of labor market manipulation that has until recently been invisible. When employers suppress wages or limit labor mobility by coordinating their wage-setting and hiring practices, they should face liability. The franchise form should not be a Get Out of Jail Free card for large businesses. Congress should tighten up the antitrust laws so that employers with massive labor market power are presumptively liable when they engage in anticompetitive labor practices. Courts and lawyers can do their part as well by using the latest economic wisdom to evaluate labor monopsony cases. Lawyers can show more creativity in identifying workplace policies that reduce competition, and courts should be open to creative arguments. The FTC and the DOJ should review mergers for labor market effects. Noncompetes should be scrutinized under the antitrust laws; the traditional common law approach is inadequate. And Congress should block employers from using arbitration clauses to protect themselves from antitrust class actions. Much more along these lines can be done, as I suggested in earlier chapters.

Legal academics also need to catch up. The imbalance between product-market litigation and labor-market litigation is matched by an imbalance in legal research on product-market antitrust (which is voluminous) and legal research on labor-market antitrust (which is paltry). It is still common to think that labor markets are more or less competitive, while the better paradigm is one of monopsonistic competition. As this paradigm takes hold and disseminates through the legal culture, courts and regulators will (or should) be more responsive to challenges to conventional employment practices. Rethinking needs to be done, and not just about antitrust law. In a world of pervasive monopsonistic labor market competition, employment and labor law will not only be stronger than it is now. It will look different as well.

***

While my argument has rested on traditional understandings of labor markets and the role of antitrust law for regulating markets, in the past few years we have been told that work is undergoing a rapid transformation and the old rules will no longer apply. This raises the question of whether antitrust law is a dinosaur or (to mix metaphors) remains a useful tool for regulating modern labor markets.

The argument that labor markets are undergoing radical change actually reflects two different sets of anxieties and points to a different set of developments. The first argument can be called the "gig economy" challenge. Technological developments have given firms new powers to manipulate workers, allowing employers to suppress pay and benefits. Firms can contract out more easily than in the past and set up platforms for matching workers and customers that strip workers of traditional protections. The result has been a hollowing-out of the middle class and the extension of new burdens and indignities on the working poor.[1]

The second argument is more radical and a little scary. As artificial intelligence (AI) develops, a large class of unemployable people will be created, people whose skills no longer have any market value because AI replicates those skills at less cost. The world will be one in which a handful of people own all the machines—the robots that produce the goods and services and the robots that make and repair robots—and everyone else will be superfluous.

The first argument overstates modern developments and the rupture with the past. There is no doubt that technology has enabled firms to reorganize their relationships with workers. But these changes have been subtle, and taking the long view, they are a continuation of labor market experimentation that goes back more than a century.[2] Employers have always relied on a mix of employees and independent contractors and have frequently adjusted that mix in response to technological changes. Labor relations have always been quite fluid—except when firms and unions were able to lock in a set of arrangements for a time. The modern push toward contractor status is partly driven by efforts of employers to avoid employment law protections, and where that is the case, misclassification litigation is the proper response. Newly flexible work arrangements that allow people to work part time and from home are a boon for many people even if such jobs may be dead ends for those who are unable to find full-time jobs. The establishment of platforms that allow workers to match with customers seems like a welcome development. If the platforms are well designed, the workers will compete with each other for customers, and customers will compete for workers. The high level of choice on both sides should protect both sides of the platform from anticompetitive behavior. The platform owner, given market power by its position, may attempt to charge excessive prices to one or both sides of the platform. It is possible that price and other forms of regulation are warranted, and antitrust authorities should scrutinize attempts to extend platform monopolies to new markets. But there is nothing wrong with the (so far modest) shift of workers from employee status to independent contractor status so long as this shift reflects market realities—and in particular, the declining significance of relationship-specific investment—rather than misclassification.

The AI revolution raises greater challenges. Already quite a few workers have lost their jobs to robots, and it appears that—contrary to earlier, more optimistic expectations—the labor market has not replaced those jobs.[3] Some commentators envision a future in which human labor no longer has any value as machines perform work more cheaply and efficiently than humans do. Just as robots have replaced welders, drivers, and agricultural workers, they will replace lawyers, accountants, and doctors. If this is true, then antitrust law will not have much of a role to play. The major challenge for public policy will be how to distribute the enormous machine-created economic surplus to ordinary people whose skills are no longer valued, and how to reconcile people to a world where they can no longer depend on work to confer dignity and meaning to their lives.[4] The question of whether this can be done has been debated for at least a century. A world run by machines would generate so much economic surplus that ordinary people would be able to live their lives without working or working much. Both history and common experience suggest that people can live meaningful lives without being tied to an office or factory; it is only recently that the cultural meaning of work was transformed from drudgery or even punishment for the sins of our ancestors to a life-affirming source of personal value. But people would need to claim a fair portion of the surplus from the owners of capital, who might otherwise horde it.

A more realistic possibility, at least in the short to medium term, is that AI will provide employers new tools for monitoring and controlling their workers. Imagine, for example, that AI enables an employer to estimate workers' reservation wage or predict if a worker is about to quit; if so, the employer might be able to maximize its profits by paying all workers their reservation wages. This would generate greater output for the economy and even less equity for workers. AI could also improve the productivity (and hence wages) of some workers while rendering other workers superfluous. This could result in greater social wealth but higher inequality than ever. A creative role for antitrust law will remain in such a world. But the real solutions lie in the realm of political philosophy and public morality.

ACKNOWLEDGMENTS

—◆—

This book is derived from several papers that I wrote alone or with colleagues. See *The Antitrust Challenge to Covenants Not to Compete in Employment Contracts*, 83 ANTITRUST L. J. 165 (2020); *Antitrust Remedies for Labor Market Power*, 132 HARVARD L. REV. 536 (2018) (with Suresh Naidu and E. Glen Weyl); *Labor Monopsony and the Limits of the Law*, J. HUM. RESOURCES (2020) (with Suresh Naidu); *Why Has Antitrust Law Failed Workers?*, 105 CORNELL L. REV. 1343 (2020) (with Ioana Marinescu). I am grateful to Marinescu, Naidu, and Weyl for collaborating with me on the earlier papers, and also for their patient advice. Many of the ideas that made their way into this book originated with them, though all errors are mine. Thanks also to Sima Biondi, Michael Christ, and Candice Yandam for their comments and research help, and to Dave McBride, my editor at Oxford, who provided encouragement and helpful comments.

NOTES

Introduction

1. *See* David Autor, David Dorn, Lawrence F. Katz, Christina Patterson & John Van Reenen, *The Fall of the Labor Share and the Rise of Superstar Firms*, 135 Q. J. ECON. 645 (2020). A recent paper attributes the decline in labor's share of output to a reduction in worker power—caused by the decline in unionization, more aggressive cost-cutting measures by employers, foreign competition from low-wage countries, and the like— but not from a rise in labor monopsony. *See* Anna Stansbury & Lawrence H. Summers, *The Declining Worker Power Hypothesis: An Explanation for the Recent Evolution of the American Economy*, NBER Working Paper No. 27193 (2020). Other work also finds no evidence that labor market concentration levels have changed over the past several decades. *See* Ben Lipsius, *Labor Market Concentration Does Not Explain the Falling Labor Share* (unpub., 2018).

2. *See* Jordan Weissman, *Disability Insurance: America's $124 Billion Secret Welfare Program*, ATLANTIC, Mar. 25, 2013, https://www.theatlantic.com/business/archive/2013/03/disability-insurance-americas-124-billion-secret-welfare-program/274302/.

3. Suresh Naidu, Eric A. Posner & Glen Weyl, *Antitrust Remedies for Labor Market Power*, 132 HARV. L. REV. 536 (2018).

4. Germán Gutiérrez & Thomas Philippon, *Declining Competition and Investment in the U.S.*, NBER Working Paper No. 23583 (2017).

5. As also noted in Ioana Marinescu & Herbert Hovenkamp, *Anticompetitive Mergers in Labor Markets*, 94 INDIANA L.J. 1031 (2019). The authors urge

regulators to take the labor market effects of mergers seriously, and discuss the analytical issues. *See also* Herbert Hovenkamp, *Whatever Did Happen to the Antitrust Movement?*, 94 NOTRE DAME L. REV. 583 (2018). A related point is that monopsony in general—including market power over inputs that are products rather than labor—has also received less attention, legally and in commentary, than sell-side anticompetitive behavior, with some people arguing that buy-side harms are legally actionable only if there is an independent harm in the output market. For a discussion and criticism of this view, see C. Scott Hemphill & Nancy L. Rose, *Mergers That Harm Sellers*, 127 YALE L.J. 2078 (2018).

6. U.S. Dep't of Justice & Federal Trade Comm'n, *Horizontal Merger Guidelines* § 1 (2010) ("To evaluate whether a merger is likely to enhance market power on the buying side of the market, the Agencies employ essentially the framework described above for evaluating whether a merger is likely to enhance market power on the selling side of the market.").

7. The only major case in recent years where the labor market effects of a merger were considered is United States v. Anthem, Inc., 855 F.3d 345 (D.C. Cir. 2017), cert. dismissed, 137 S. Ct. 2250 (2017), where a court of appeals affirmed the district court's injunction against a merger because of its anticompetitive product market effects, but the government also argued that the merger would have anticompetitive labor market effects, as recognized by the dissent. Id. at 377 (Kavanaugh, J., dissenting).

8. ADAM SMITH, AN INQUIRY INTO THE NATURE AND CAUSES OF THE WEALTH OF NATIONS 82–85 (1976).

9. For a discussion, see Clayton J. Masterman, *The Customer Is Not Always Right*, 69 VAND. L. REV. 1387 (2016).

10. DENNIS W. CARLTON & JEFFREY M. PERLOFF, MODERN INDUSTRIAL ORGANIZATION 108 (4th ed. 2005).

11. Fed. R. Civ. P. 23.

12. *See, e.g.,* Weisfeld v. Sun Chem. Corp., 84 Fed.Appx. 257 (3d Cir. 2004).

13. *See* United States v. eBay, Inc., 968 F.Supp.2d 1030 (N.D. Cal. 2013); In re High Tech Emp. Antitrust Litig., 985 F.Supp.2d 1167 (N.D. Cal. 2013); Garrison v. Oracle Corp., 159 F.Supp.3d 1044 (N.D. Cal. 2016). And, relatedly, In re Animation Workers Antitrust Litig., 123 F.Supp.3d 1175 (N.D. Cal. 2015).

14. U.S. Dep't of Justice & Federal Trade Comm'n, *Antitrust Guidance for Human Resource Professionals* (2016).

15. White House, *Non-Compete Agreements: Analysis of the Usage, Potential Issues, and State Responses* (2016); U.S. Dep't of the Treasury, Office of Econ. Pol'y, *Non-Compete Contracts: Economic Effects and Policy Implications* (2016).

16. Dave Jamieson, *Jimmy John's Makes Low-Wage Workers Sign "Oppressive" Noncompete Agreements*, HUFFINGTON POST (2014), https://www.

huffingtonpost.com/2014/10/13/jimmy-johns-non-compete_n_5978180.
html.

17. Evan Starr, J. J. Prescott, & Norman Bishara, *Noncompetes in the U.S. Labor Force* (unpub., 2017), https://papers.ssrn.com/sol3/papers.cfm?abstract_id=2625714.

18. Alan B. Krueger & Orley Ashenfelter, *Theory and Evidence on Employer Collusion in the Franchise Sector,* Princeton University Working Paper No. 614 (Sept. 28, 2017).

19. Conor Dougherty, *How Noncompete Clauses Keep Workers Locked In,* N.Y. TIMES, May 13, 2017; Conor Dougherty, *Noncompete Pacts, under Siege, Find Haven in Idaho,* N.Y. TIMES, July 14, 2017.

20. David Card & Alan B. Krueger, *Minimum Wages and Employment: A Case Study of the Fast-Food Industry in New Jersey and Pennsylvania,* 90 AMER. ECON. REV. 1397 (2000).

21. *See* Arindrajit Dube, T. William Lester, & Michael Reich, *Minimum Wage Shocks, Employment Flows, and Labor Market Frictions,* 34 J. LAB. ECON. 663 (2016).

Chapter 1

1. JOAN ROBINSON, THE ECONOMICS OF IMPERFECT COMPETITION (1933); Robert J. Thornton, *Retrospectives: How Joan Robinson and B. L. Hallward Named Monopsony,* 18 J. ECON. PERSP. 257 (2004).

2. ADAM SMITH, AN INQUIRY INTO THE NATURE AND CAUSES OF THE WEALTH OF NATIONS 70–71 (1776).

3. Marx discussed this concept, originally coined by Friedrich Engels, in numerous works, including KARL MARX, CAPITAL: A CRITIQUE OF POLITICAL ECONOMY, vol. 1 (Ben Fowkes trans., 1992).

4. Lloyd Reynolds, *The Supply of Labor to the Firm,* 60 Q. J. ECON. 390 (1946); Lloyd G. Reynolds, *Wage Differences in Local Labor Markets,* 36 AMER. ECON. REV. 366 (1946).

5. E.g., Fair Labor Standards Act of 1938, ch. 676, 52 Stat. 1060 (codified as amended at 29 U.S.C. §§ 201–219, 557 (2012)).

6. National Labor Relations Act of 1935, ch. 372, 49 Stat. 449 (codified as amended at 29 U.S.C. §§ 151–169).

7. 15 U.S.C. §§ 1–7 (2012).

8. James Albrecht, *Search Theory: The 2010 Nobel Memorial Prize in Economic Sciences,* 113 SCANDINAVIAN J. ECON. 237 (2011).

9. Kenneth Burdett & Dale T. Mortensen, *Wage Differentials, Employer Size, and Unemployment,* 39 INT'L ECON. REV. 257 (1998).

10. *See* ALAN MANNING, MONOPSONY IN MOTION: IMPERFECT COMPETITION IN LABOR MARKETS (2003); Alan Manning, *Imperfect Competition in the Labor Market,* in 4B HANDBOOK OF LAB. ECON. 973 (2011).

11. *See* Venkataraman Bhaskar & Ted To, *Minimum Wages for Ronald McDonald Monopsonies: A Theory of Monopsonistic Competition,* 109

Econ. J. 190 (1999); David Card, Ana Rute Cardoso, Joerg Heining & Patrick Kline, *Firms and Labor Market Inequality: Evidence and Some Theory*, 36 J. Lab. Econ. S. 13 (2018).

12. *See* Sanford M. Jacoby, Employing Bureaucracy: Managers, Unions, and the Transformation of Work in American Industry, 1900–1945, ch. 5 (1985).

13. *Id.* at 49-52.

14. *Id.* at 50.

15. Samuel Bowles & Herbert Gintis, Schooling in Capitalist America: Educational Reform of Economic Life (1976).

16. Michael Burawoy, Manufacturing Consent: Changes in the Labor Process under Monopoly Capitalism (1979).

17. *See* Rick Fantasia, *From Class Consciousness to Culture, Action, and Social Organization*, 21 Ann. Rev. Socio. 1, 269 (1995); Arlie Russell Hochschild, The Managed Heart: Commercialization of Human Feeling (1983).

18. *See, e.g.,* Suresh Naidu, Yaw Nyarko & Shing-Yi Wang, *Monopsony Power in Migrant Labor Markets: Evidence from the United Arab Emirates*, J. Pol. Econ. 1735 (2016); Efraim Benmelech, Nittai Bergman & Hyunseob Kim, *Strong Employers and Weak Employees: How Does Employer Concentration Affect Wages?*, NBER Working Paper No. 24307 (2018); José Azar, Ioana Marinescu & Marshall Steinbaum, *Labor Market Concentration*, NBER Working Paper No. 24147 (2019); Kevin Rinz, *Labor Market Concentration, Earnings Inequality, and Earnings Mobility, Center for Economic Studies,* US Census Bureau Working Paper 2018-10, 30 (2018); David Arnold, *Mergers and Acquisitions, Local Labor Market Concentration, and Worker Outcomes* (unpub., 2019); Ben Lipsius, Labor Market Concentration Does Not Explain the Falling Labor Share (unpub., 2018); Brad Hershbein, Claudia Macaluso & Chen Yeh, *Concentration in U.S. Local Labor Markets: Evidence from Vacancy and Employment Data* at 12–13 (unpub., 2018).

19. I omit one potential source of monopsony that has been proposed but not explored empirically, adverse selection in the market for workers who want to quit, as in Daron Acemoglu & Jörn-Steffen Pischke, *Why Do Firms Train? Theory and Evidence*, 113 Q. J. Econ. 79, 80, 113 (1998).

20. Economists have combined some of these models into single "hybrid" models. *See, e.g.,* David Berger, Kyle Herkenhoff & Simon Mongey, *Labor Market Power*, NBER Working Paper No. 25719 (2018), https://www.nber.org/papers/w25719.

21. Catherine Rampell, *Two from U.S. Win Nobel in Economics*, N.Y. Times, Oct. 15, 2012, http://www.nytimes.com/2012/10/16/business/economy/alvin-roth-and-lloyd-shapley-win-nobel-in-economic-science.html.

22. *See, e.g.,* David Card, Alexandre Mas, Enrico Moretti & Emmanuel Saez, *Inequality at Work: The Effect of Peer Salaries on Job Satisfaction*, 102

AM. ECON. REV. 2981 (2012). To be sure, some wage discrimination does take place, just as some price discrimination takes place, but it takes a crude and rudimentary form, for example, wage discrimination based on gender, where presumably employers are able to generalize based on rough correlations between reservation wages and sex. *See* David Card, Ana Rute Cardoso & Patrick Kline, *Bargaining, Sorting, and the Gender Wage Gap: Quantifying the Impact of Firms on the Relative Pay of Women*, 132 Q. J. ECON. 633 (2015).

23. For the complete analysis of monopsony in labor markets, *see,* e.g., Manning, *supra* note 10.

24. *See* Raj Chetty, *Bounds on Elasticities with Optimization Frictions: A Synthesis of Micro and Macro Evidence on Labor Supply*, 80 ECONOMETRICA 969, 1015 (2012). For a more recent review, see Michael Keane & Richard Rogerson, *Reconciling Micro and Macro Labor Supply Elasticities: A Structural Perspective*, 7 ANN. REV. ECON. 89, 114 (2015).

25. *See infra* pp. 26–27.

26. Michael Spence has highlighted an analogous distortion in the product market. A. Michael Spence, *Monopoly, Quality and Regulation*, 6 BELL J. ECON. 417 (1975).

27. However, if the product market is competitive, prices for consumers will not rise. The reduced sales of the monopsonist will be offset by the sales of new firms that enter the product market.

28. *See* William M. Boal & Michael R. Ransom, *Monopsony in the Labor Market*, 25 J. ECON. LIT. 86 (1997).

29. William M. Boal, *Testing for Employer Monopsony in Turn-of-the-Century Coal Mining*, 26 RAND J. ECON. 519 (1995).

30. *See* Boal & Ransom, *infra* note 33.

31. Statute of Labourers 1351, 25 Edw. 3c. 1–7 (Eng.); see also Ordinance of Labourers 1349, 23 Edw. 3 c. 1–7 (Eng.).

32. *See* KAREN ORREN, BELATED FEUDALISM: LABOR, THE LAW, AND LIBERAL DEVELOPMENT IN THE UNITED STATES (1991); CHRISTOPHER L. TOMLINS, LAW, LABOR, AND IDEOLOGY IN THE EARLY AMERICAN REPUBLIC (1993).

33. Suresh Naidu, *Recruitment Restrictions and Labor Markets: Evidence from the Postbellum U.S. South*, 28 J. LAB. ECON. 413 (2010).

34. *See* Suresh Naidu & Noam Yuchtman, *Labor Market Institutions in the Gilded Age of American Economic History* 5–7, 6–20, NBER Working Paper No. 22117 (2016) for evidence that 19th-century Northern labor markets were monopsonistic and that the violent conflict of the period was over these labor market rents.

35. ALEX GOUREVITCH, FROM SLAVERY TO THE COOPERATIVE COMMONWEALTH: LABOR AND REPUBLICAN LIBERTY IN THE NINETEENTH CENTURY 106–16 (2015).

36. *See,* e.g., Ernesto Dal Bó, Frederico Finan & Martín A. Ross, *Strengthening State Capabilities: The Role of Financial Incentives in the Call*

to Public Service, 128 Q. J. Econ. 1169 (2013). The authors randomized advertised wages for government jobs in Mexico and found that the Mexican government possessed a significant degree of monopsony power, with labor supply elasticity of 2.15, comparable to the findings of studies of monopsony power that did not use randomization.

37. Much of the earlier work focused on the market for nursing because of antitrust litigation against hospitals. The results were mixed, likely because of data limitations that the more recent work, discussed below, has made progress on. *See,* e.g., Janet Currie, Mehdi Farsi & W. Bentley Macleod, *Cut to the Bone? Hospital Takeovers and Nurse Employment Contracts*, 58 Indus. & Lab. Rel. Rev. 494 (2005) (and citations therein).

38. David Card, Lawrence F. Katz & Alan B. Krueger, Comment on David Neumark & William Wascher, *Employment Effects of Minimum and Subminimum Wages: Panel Data on State Minimum Wage Laws*, 47 Indus. & Lab. Rel. Rev. 487 (1994).

39. Arindrajit Dube, Suresh Naidu & Michael Reich, *The Economic Effects of a Citywide Minimum Wage*, 60 Indus. & Lab. Rel. Rev. 522 (2007).

40. Arindrajit Dube, T. William Lester & Michael Reich, *Minimum Wage Shocks, Employment Flows, and Labor Market Frictions*, 34 J. Lab. Econ. 663 (2016).

41. See Douglas A. Webber, *Firm Market Power and the Earnings Distribution*, 35 Lab. Econ. 123 (2015); Douglas A. Webber, *Firm-Level Monopsony and the Gender Pay Gap*, 55 Ind. Relat. 323 (2016); Sydnee Caldwell & Emily Oehlsen, *Monopsony and the Gender Wage Gap: Experimental Evidence from the Gig Economy* (unpub., 2018); Arindrajit Dube, Laura Giuliano & Jonathan Leonard, *Fairness and Frictions: The Impact of Unequal Raises on Quit Behavior*, NBER Working Paper 24906 (2018); Arindrajit Dube, Jeff Jacobs, Suresh Naidu & Siddharth Suri, *Monopsony in Online Labor Markets*, NBER Working Paper 24416 (2018); Arindrajit Dube, Alan Manning & Suresh Naidu, "Monopsony and Employer Mis-optimization Explain Why Wages Bunch at Round Numbers." NBER Working Paper 24991 (2018); Ihsaan Bassier, Arindrajit Dube & Suresh Naidu, *Monopsony in Movers: The Elasticity of Labor Supply to Firm Wage Policies* (unpub., 2019); David E. Card, Ana Rute Cardoso & Joerg Heining, *Firms and Labor Market Inequality: Evidence and Some Theory*, 36 J. Lab. Econ. S13 (2016); Patrick Kline, Neviana Petkova, Heidi Williams & Owen Zidar, *Who Profits from Patents? Rent-Sharing at Innovative Firms*, Inst. for Research on Lab. & Employment, Working Paper No. 107-17 (2017).

42. Alan Manning & Barbara Petrongolo, *How Local Are Labor Markets? Evidence from a Spatial Job Search Model*, 107 Am. Econ. Rev. 2877 (2017).

43. Ioana Marinescu & Roland Rathelot, *Mismatch Unemployment and The Geography of Job Search*, NBER Working Paper No. 22672 (2017), https://www.nber.org/papers/w22672.pdf.

44. José Azar et al., *Concentration in US labor markets: Evidence from online vacancy data*, 66 LAB. ECON. 101886 (2020) .

45. Efraim Benmelech, Nittai Bergman & Hyunseob Kim, *Strong Employers and Weak Employees: How Does Employer Concentration Affect Wages?*, NBER Working Paper No. 24037 (2018), https://www.nber.org/papers/w24147.pdf.

46. See also Kevin Rinz, *Labor Market Concentration, Earnings Inequality, and Earnings Mobility, Center for Economic Studies,* US Census Bureau Working Paper 2018-10, 30 (2018); David Arnold, *Mergers and Acquisitions, Local Labor Market Concentration, and Worker Outcomes* (unpub., 2019); Ben Lipsius, Labor Market Concentration Does Not Explain the Falling Labor Share (unpub., 2018); Brad Hershbein, Claudia Macaluso & Chen Yeh, *Concentration in U.S. Local Labor Markets: Evidence from Vacancy and Employment Data* 12–13 (unpub., 2018).

47. David Berger, Kyle Herkenhoff & Simon Mongey, *Labor Market Power*, NBER Working Paper No. 25719 (2021), https://www.nber.org/papers/w25719.

48. Suresh Naidu, Eric A. Posner & Glen Weyl, *Antitrust Remedies for Labor Market Power*, 132 HARV. L. REV. 536 (2018), and see online appendix.

Chapter 2

1. 15 U.S.C. § 1 (2004).
2. 15 U.S.C. § 2 (2004).
3. *Id.*
4. Weyerhaeuser Co. v. Ross-Simmons Hardwood Lumber Co., 549 U.S. 312 (2007).
5. 15 U.S.C. § 17 (1914); *see also* 29 U.S.C. § 52 (1914); a related nonstatutory exemption was recognized in Brown v. Pro Football, Inc., 518 U.S. 231 (1996).
6. *See,* e.g., Mineral Water Bottle Exchange & Trade Protection Soc. v. Booth, 36 Ch. D. 465 (1887), which involved an agreement among almost 200 employers not to hire each other's former employees for a period of time; Huston v. Reutlinger, 91 Ky. 333, 15 S.W. 867 (1891), which involved an agreement to fix wages, among other things.
7. Anderson v. Shipowners' Ass'n of Pac. Coast, 272 U.S. 359 (1926).
8. *See,* e.g., Kartell v. Blue Shield of Mass., 749 F.2d 922, 924–25 (1st Cir. 1984) (Breyer, J.); Banks v. Nat'l Collegiate Athletic Ass'n, 977 F.2d 1081, 1084 (7th Cir. 1992).
9. U.S. Dep't of Justice & Federal Trade Comm'n, Horizontal Merger Guidelines (2010).
10. *Federal Trade Commission Staff Submission to Texas Health and Human Services Commission regarding the Certificate of Public Advantage Applications of Hendrick Health System and Shannon Health System* 36–38

(Sept. 11, 2020), https://www.ftc.gov/system/files/documents/advocacy_
documents/ftc-staff-comment-texas-health-human-services-commission-
regarding-certificate-public-advantage/20100902010119texashhsccopacom
ment.pdf.

11. *See also* Herbert Hovenkamp, *Whatever Did Happen to the Antitrust Movement?*, 93 NOTRE DAME L. REV. 583 (2018).

12. U.S. Dep't of Justice, Office of Public Affairs, *Justice Department Requires Six High Tech Companies to Stop Entering into Anticompetitive Employee Solicitation Agreements* (Sept. 24, 2010), https://www.justice.gov/opa/pr/justice-department-requires-six-high-tech-companies-stop-entering-anticompetitive-employee.

13. U.S. Dep't of Justice & Federal Trade Comm'n, *Antitrust Guidance for Human Resource Professionals* (2016).

14. *See* Alan B. Krueger & Eric A. Posner, *Hamilton Project: A Proposal for Protecting Low-Income Workers from Monopsony and Collusion* 11–12 The Brookings Institution (2018).

15. Rachel Abrams, *Why Aren't Paychecks Growing? A Burger-Joint Clause Offers a Clue*, N.Y. TIMES, Sept. 27, 2017.

16. Mark L. Krotoski, *DOJ Antitrust Division Announces Imminent Criminal Prosecution for "No Poaching" Agreements*, NAT. L. REV. (Feb. 6, 2018).

17. Gustavo Grullon, Yelena Larkin & Roni Michaely, *Are US Industries Becoming More Concentrated?* (unpub., 2017); Gauti B. Eggertsson, Jacob A. Robbins & Ella Getz Wold, *Kaldor and Piketty's Facts: The Rise of Monopoly Power in the United States*, NBER Working Paper No. 24287 (2018), https://www.nber.org/papers/w24287.pdf.

18. *See* J. T. Prince & D. H. Simon, *The Impact of Mergers on Quality Provision: Evidence from the Airline Industry*, 65 J. IND. ECON. 336 (2017).

19. Janet Currie, Medhi Farsi & Bentley MacLeod, *Cut to the Bone? Hospital Takeovers and Nurse Employment Contracts*, 53 ILR REV. 471 (2005).

20. Christopher Doering, *Who Will Food Industry Consolidation Squeeze?*, USA Today, June 5, 2014, https://www.usatoday.com/story/money/business/2014/06/05/food-companies-mergers/9926501/.

21. In 2017 TaskRabbit was acquired by IKEA, and in early 2018 WorkMarket was acquired by ADP. Jason D. Rowley, *Fiverr's AND CO Acquisition Continues Freelance Consolidation Trend*, CRUNCHBASE NEWS, Jan. 24, 2018, https://news.crunchbase.com/news/fiverrs-co-acquisition-continues-freelance-consolidation-trend/.

22. Alan Manning & Barbara Petrongolo, *How Local Are Labor Markets? Evidence from a Spatial Job Search Model*, 107 AM. ECON. REV. 2877 (2017).

23. *See* José Azar et al., *Concentration in US labor markets: Evidence from online vacancy data*, 66 LAB. ECON. Table 1 (2020).

24. *Id.*

25. *Id.* at 3.

26. E.g., In re NCAA Walk-on Litigation, 398 F. Supp. 2d 1144, 1150 (W.D.WA 2005) (incorrectly referring to the labor market as a product market).

27. Todd v. Exxon Corp., 126 F. Supp. 2d 321, 325 (S.D.N.Y. 2000).

28. E.g., Helmerich & Payne Int'l Drilling Co. v. Schlumberger Tech. Corp., 17-CV-358-GKF-FHM, 2017 WL 6597512, at *5 (N.D. Okla. Dec. 26, 2017) ("[. . .] Complaint is silent as to the geographic market, and includes no facts upon which an inference of the relevant geographic market may be based.").

29. Todd v. Exxon, 275 F.3d 191. 199, 202.

30. See, e.g., Hanger v. Berkley Group, 5:13-cv-113 2015 WL 3439255, at *10–11 (dismissing case because plaintiffs failed to defend geographic scope of market); Helmerich & Payne, 2017 WL 6597512, at *5 (N.D. Okla. Dec. 26, 2017) (dismissing the claim because the plaintiff's labor market definition—"specialized engineers"—was insufficiently specific, failed to refer to the interchangeability of the engineers working for each firm, and lacked a geographic market); Mooney v. AXA Advisors, L.L.C., 19 F.Supp.3d 486, 499 (S.D. NY 2014) (rejecting labor market definition because of lack of "discussion about the insurance agent labor supply, the existence of other insurance agents that are not affiliated with AXA, potential barriers to entry into the insurance agent market, or systemic barriers that might prevent an agent from changing insurance employers").

31. Eichorn v. AT&T Corp., 248 F.3d 131, 147–48 (3d Cir. 2001). But see Cason-Merenda v. Detroit Med. Ctr., 862 F. Supp. 2d 603, 647 (E.D. Mich. 2012), where the court recognized that a labor market could be composed of nurses who work for hospitals and not, as the defendant argued, nurses who work for non-hospitals as well; Rock v. NCAA, 2013 WL 4479815 at *14 (S.D.Ind. 2013).

32. Consider, for example, Maderazo v. VHS San Antonio Partners, L.P., 2019 WL 4254633 (W.D. Tex. Jan. 22, 2019), where a court denied a motion for class certification because it believed that the experts failed to establish causation—that the alleged wage-fixing conspiracy caused harm to the class members. The real grounds for the court's decision was not class certification—obviously, causation is a common issue—but failure of proof of causation. The problem was that while the experts could show that the wages were lower than the competitive level, they could not tie the wage reduction to a specific act—since the allegation was that the defendants had held numerous meetings over a period of time during which they negotiated wage commitments. But it is hard to see how any wage-fixing case (or even price-fixing case) could survive this judge's skepticism. For a more mundane example of judicial caution in light of uncertainty, see Paul Gift, UFC Hearing: Judge Calls for Expert Witness and Joe Silva Questioning, FORBES, Dec, 20, 2018, https://www.

forbes.com/sites/paulgift/2018/12/20/ufc-hearing-judge-calls-for-expert-witness-joe-silva-questioning-mma-news/#4dca24119024 [https://perma.cc/4MRJ-XYQE].

33. One study found, based on a sample of 40 large cases that led to a recovery, that 26 of those cases were initiated by the government. *See* Robert H. Lande and Joshua P. Davis, *Benefits from Private Antitrust Enforcement: An Analysis of Forty Cases*, 42 U.S.F. L. Rev. 879, 898 (2008).

34. Bryan Koenig, *DOJ Gives Fast-Food Chains Ammo against No-Poach Suits*, Law 360, Jan. 29, 2019, https://www.law360.com/articles/1123203/doj-gives-fast-food-chains-ammo-against-no-poach-suits [https://perma.cc/3HPZ-MKVW].

35. *See* Economic Analysis Group, Department of Justice, https://www.justice.gov/atr/about-division/economic-analysis-group.

36. *See* Horizontal Merger Guidelines, supra note 9.

37. *See* Minn. Ass'n of Nurse Anesthetists v. Unity Hosp., 208 F.3d 655, 658, 659 (8th Cir. 2000) ("[P]laintiffs assert that the sole-source contracts were part of a 'grand conspiracy' by Minnesota anesthesiologists" to eliminate competition in the Twin Cities.).

38. *See, e.g.,* White v. R. M. Packer Co., Inc., 635 F.3d 571, 574 (1st Cir. 2011) ("[P]laintiffs in this case complain that the prices for gasoline on Martha's Vineyard have been artificially high due . . . to an illegal price-fixing conspiracy."); In re Digital Music Antitrust Litigation, 812 F. Supp. 2d 390, 397 (S.D. NY 2011) ("Plaintiffs allege that Defendants' motive to conspire was to support their ability to charge supracompetitive prices.").

39. Weisfeld v. Sun Chem. Corp., 210 F.R.D. 136, 144 (D.N.J. 2002), aff'd, 84 Fed. Appx. 257, 257 (3d Cir. 2004). *See also* Todd v. Exxon, 275 F.3d 191, 202 n.5 (noting the difficulties that plaintiffs will face in obtaining class certification because of differences among class members). *See also* Maderazo v. VHS San Antonio Partners, L.P., Civil Action No. SA-06-CA-535-OG, 24 (Jan. 22, 2019), https://images.law.com/contrib/content/uploads/documents/401/15176/Maderazo-Class-Cert-Ruling.pdf [https://perma.cc/TCW9-UUEP] (denying class certification because experts could not prove causal impact of alleged conspiracy); Fleischman v. Albany Medical Center, No. 1:06-CV-765, 2008 WL 2945993, *6 (N.D.N.Y. July 28, 2008) ("Interchangeability and job mobility in the nursing profession, and the reasons affecting the wage of a particular nurse or class of nurses, though contested, involve too many variables and provide too much ambiguity to carry a motion for class certification on the issue of injury-in-fact."); Reed v. Advocate Health Care, 268 F.R.D. 573, 592, 594 (N.D. Ill. 2009) (denying class certification because of variation in wages paid to class members); In re Comp. of Managerial, Prof'l, & Technical Emps. Antitrust Litig., No. 02-2924, 2003 WL

26115698, at *4 (D.N.J. May 27, 2003) (similar). However, other courts disagree. *See,* e.g., In re High-Tech Employee Antitrust Litig., 985 F. Supp. 2d 1167, 1183 n.8 (N.D. Cal. 2013).

40. Nitsch et al. v. Dreamworks Animation SKG Inc., 315 F.R.D. 270 (N.D. Cal. 2016) (animation workers); In re High-Tech Employee Antitrust Litigation, 985 F. Supp. 2d 1167 (N.D. Cal. 2013) (high-tech employees); Cason-Merenda v. VHS of Michigan, Inc., 296 F.R.D. 528 (E.D. Mich. 2013) (nurse wages—Detroit); Cason-Merenda v. VHS of Michigan, Inc., No. 06-15601, 2014 U.S. Dist. LEXIS 29447 (E.D. Mich. Mar. 7, 2014) (reinstating class certification order on remand following Sixth Circuit post-Comcast reversal); Fleischman v. Albany Medical Center, No. 06-cv-0765, 2008 U.S. Dist. LEXIS 57188 (N.D.N.Y. July 28, 2008) (nurse wages—Albany).

41. *See* Michael Selmi & Sylvia Tsakos, *Employment Discrimination Class Actions after Wal-Mart v. Dukes,* 48 AKRON L. REV. 803, 830 (2015) (noting that lower courts that remain sympathetic to class action claims for employment discrimination find ways around *Wal-Mart*).

42. *See* Council of Econ. Advisers, Exec. Office of the President, Benefits of Competition and Indicators of Market Power, at 13 (Apr. 2016).

43. I have heard this explanation in conversations with private litigators who have been involved in labor monopsony cases.

44. Am. Exp. Co. v. Italian Colors Rest., 570 U.S. 228, 234 (2013).

45. For a rare example, *see* Aya Healthcare Servs., Inc. v. AMN Healthcare, Inc., No. 17CV205-MMA (MDD), 2018 WL 3032552, at *3 (S.D. Cal. June 19, 2018).

46. Henry Farber, Dan Herbst, Ilyana Kuziemko & Suresh Naidu, *Unions and Inequality in the 20th Century: New Evidence from Survey Data* (unpub., 2018).

47. David Weil, THE FISSURED WORKPLACE: WHY WORK BECAME SO BAD FOR SO MANY AND WHAT CAN BE DONE TO IMPROVE IT (2017); Lawrence F. Katz & Alan B. Krueger, *The Rise and Nature of Alternative Work Arrangements in the United States,* NBER Working Paper No. 22667 (2016), https://www.nber.org/papers/w22667.pdf. On the relationship between monopsony and outsourcing, *see* Arindrajit Dube & Ethan Kaplan, *Does Outsourcing Reduce Wages in the Low-Wage Service Occupations? Evidence from Janitors and Guards,* 63.2 IND. & LAB. REL. REV. 287 (2010); Deborah Goldschmidt & Johannes F. Schmieder, *The Rise of Domestic Outsourcing and the Evolution of the German Wage Structure,* 132 Q. J. ECON. 1165 (2017).

Chapter 3

1. Llacua v. W. Range Ass'n, 930 F.3d 1161 (10th Cir. 2019).
2. *Id.* at 1180.
3. *Id.* at 1181.

4. The opinion contrasts with Beltran v. InterExchange, Inc., 176 F.Supp.3d 1066 (2016) (D.Col. 2016), where the court denied the motion to dismiss under a similar set of facts, except involving nannies rather than sheep herders. But the case was distinguished by a rare "smoking gun": the plaintiff's investigator was told by the director of one of the defendants that the defendants agreed to fix wages. *Id.* at 1074. Such direct evidence of conspiracy is extremely rare in antitrust cases.

5. *See* Nat'l. Soc. of Prof. Engineers v. United States, 435 U.S. 679, 692 (1978).

6. *See,* e.g., Broadcast Music, Inc. v. Columbia Broadcasting Sys., Inc. 441 U.S. 1, 23 (1979).

7. Based on a Westlaw search for "section /3 1 /3 sherman +1 act & product +1 market" (January 15, 2020), which yielded 74 hits for the past year, and 184 hits for the past three years.

8. *See* Fleischman v. Albany Med. Ctr., 728 F. Supp. 2d 130, 162 (N.D.N.Y. 2010) (denying motion to dismiss per se wage-fixing claim).

9. Based on a Westlaw search for "section /3 1 /3 sherman +1 act & labor +1 market" (January 15, 2020), which yielded five hits for the past year, and 18 hits for the past three years.

10. Based on a Westlaw search for "section /3 1 /3 sherman +1 act & labor +1 market & league" (January 15, 2020), which yielded three hits for the past year, and 10 for the past three years.

11. *See* O'Bannon v. Nat'l. Collegiate Athletic Ass'n., 802 F.3d 1049, 1070 (2015) (vacating the district court's judgment that required the NCAA to allow its member schools to pay student-athletes up to $5,000 per year).

12. 728 F. Supp. 2d 130, 159 (N.D.N.Y. 2010).

13. For a discussion, see Jeff Miles, *The Nursing Shortage, Wage-Information Sharing among Competing Hospitals, and the Antitrust Laws: The Nurse Wages Antitrust Litigation,* 7 Hous. J. Health L. & Pol'y 305, 306–7 (2007).

14. 126 F. Supp. 2d 321, 321 (S.D.N.Y. 2000).

15. *Id.* at 325.

16. *Id.* at 327.

17. *Id.* at 323.

18. *See* Todd v. Exxon Corp., 275 F.3d 191, 200–204, 214 (2d Cir. 2001).

19. U.S. Dep't of Justice, *Justice Department Requires Six High Tech Companies to Stop Entering into Anticompetitive Employee Solicitation Agreements* (Sept. 24, 2010).

20. In re Animation Workers Antitrust Litigation, 123 F.Supp.3d 1175, 1178 (N.D. Cal., 2015); United States v. eBay, Inc., 968 F.Supp.2d 1030, 1032 (N.D.Cal. 2013); In re High-Tech Employee Antitrust Litigation, 856 F.Supp.2d 1103, 1107–8 (N.D.Cal. 2012).

21. *See* U.S. v. eBay, Inc., 968 F. Supp. 2d at 1035–36; In re High–Tech Employee Antitrust Litigation, 856 F. Supp. 2d at 1110.

22. U.S. Dep't of Justice & Federal Trade Comm'n, *Antitrust Guidance for Human Resource Professionals* (2016).

23. Danielle SEAMAN, individually and on behalf of all others similarly situated, Plaintiff, v. DUKE UNIVERSITY, Duke University Health System; The University of North Carolina at Chapel Hill; The University of North Carolina School of Medicine; The University of North Carolina Health Care System; and William L. Roper; and Does 1-20, Defendants, 2017 WL 4877210 (M.D.N.C.), at para. 57.

24. *Id.*, at para. 58.

25. *See,* e.g., Hanger v. Berkley Group, 2015 WL 3439255 at *12 (W.D. Va. 2015) (holding that in failing to define the proper labor market, plaintiffs failed to allege a plausible claim under Section 1 of the Sherman Act); Cesnik v. Chrysler Corp., 490 F. Supp. 859, 868 (M.D. Tenn. 1980) (holding that an agreement by a corporation selling one of its divisions to not rehire any managerial employee who refused employment with the buying corporation was not a violation of the Sherman Act); *but see* Roman v. Cessna Aircraft Co., 55 F.3d 542, 543, 545 (10th Cir. 1995) (reversing district court's dismissal of antitrust complaint and holding that alleging (i) that illegal agreement was only reason plaintiff was not hired by competitor, (ii) that market for plaintiff's engineer services was impeded, and (iii) that illegal agreement prevented plaintiff from selling services to highest bidder was sufficient for antitrust standing).

26. 248 F.3d 131, 136–37 (3d Cir. 2001).

27. *Id.* at 147.

28. *Id.* at 147–48.

29. *Id.* at 148 n.5.

30. *See* Ioana Marinescu & Roland Rathelot, *Mismatch Unemployment and the Geography of Job Search*, 10 AM. ECON. J.: MACROECONOMICS 42 (July 2018); Alan Manning & Barbara Petrongolo, *How Local Are Labor Markets? Evidence from a Spatial Job Search Model*, 107 AM. ECON. REV. 2877, 2877 (2017).

31. *See,* e.g., Williams v. Nevada, 794 F. Supp. 1026, 1032–34 (D. Nev. 1992), aff'd sub nom. Williams v. I. B. Fischer Nevada, 999 F.2d 445, 446 (9th Cir. 1993) (granting motion to dismiss on Section 2 claim where the plaintiff, who complained that he was terminated without good cause by an employer who allegedly had labor market power, failed to allege an anticompetitive act).

32. *See* Am. Needle, Inc. v. Nat'l Football League, 560 U.S. 183, 191 (2010).

33. Alan B. Krueger & Orley Ashenfelter, *Theory and Evidence on Employer Collusion in the Franchise Sector*, at 21–22, Princeton University Working Paper No. 614 (Sept. 28, 2017).

34. Arrington v. Burger King Worldwide, Inc., 448 F.Supp.3d 1322 (S.D. Fla. 2020).

35. Jien et al. v. Perdue Farms et al., Civil Action No. 1:19-CV-2521 (D. Md. 2019).

36. In re Broiler Chicken Antitrust Litig., 290 F. Supp. 3d 772, 781 (N.D. Ill. 2017).

37. *See* U.S. Dep't of Justice & Federal Trade Comm'n, *Horizontal Merger Guidelines* § 7 (2010); William H. Page, *Tacit Agreement under Section 1 of the Sherman Act*, 81 ANTITRUST L. J. 593, 594–96 (2017).

38. LOUIS KAPLOW, COMPETITION POLICY AND PRICE FIXING 443–53 (2013).

39. Donald Turner, *The Definition of Agreement under the Sherman Act*, 75 HARV. L. REV. 655, 669–71 (1962).

40. Jeremy Bulow & Jonathan Levin, *Matching and Price Competition*, 96 AMER. ECON. REV. 652 (2006).

41. *See* Griggs v. Duke Power Co., 401 U.S. 424, 431–32 (1971).

42. 2017 WL 3115169, at *6 (N.D. Cal. July 21, 2017), aff'd, 2018 WL 6721730 (9th Cir. 2018).

43. *Griggs*, 401 U.S. 424, 430 n.6.

44. *See, e.g.*, Butler v. Jimmy John's Franchise, LLC, 331 F. Supp. 3d 786, 790 (S.D. Ill. 2018); Deslandes v. McDonald's USA, LLC, No. 17 C 4857, 2018 WL 3105955, at *6 (N.D. Ill. June 25, 2018).

45. *Deslandes*, 2018 WL 3105955, at *2 (brackets in original).

46. *Id.*

47. *Id.* at *3.

48. *Id.*

49. *Id.*

50. *Butler*, 331 F. Supp. 3d at 796.

51. Cont'l T.V., Inc. v. GTE Sylvania Inc., 433 U.S. 36, 54–55 (1977).

52. *See* Copperweld Corp. v. Indep. Tube Corp., 467 U.S. 752, 776 (1984).

53. Deslandes v. McDonald's USA, LLC, No. 17 C 4857, 2018 WL 3105955, at *8 (N.D. Ill. June 25, 2018).

54. *Id.* at *1.

55. *Id.* at *8.

56. It also brings the analysis of no-poaching agreements in line with the treatment of covenants not to compete, which are usually unenforceable when they are untailored and are almost always unenforceable when imposed on low-skill workers. See RESTATEMENT (SECOND) OF CONTRACTS § 188, and comments (c) and (d) (1981).

57. As suggested by the findings in Joshua D. Angrist, Sydnee Caldwell & Jonathan V. Hall, *Uber vs. Taxi: A Driver's Eye View* 1–2, NBER Working Paper No. 23891 (2017), https://www.nber.org/papers/w23891.pdf.

58. *See* Meyer v Kalanick, 174 F. Supp. 3d 817, 819–20 (S.D.N.Y. 2016), *vacated, Meyer v. Uber Technologies, Inc.*, 868 F.3d 66 (2d Cir. 2017).

Chapter 4

1. *See* José Azar et al., *Concentration in US labor market: Evidence from online vacancy data*, 66 LAB. ECON., Table 1 (2020).
2. 15 U.S.C. § 2 (2004).
3. Based on a Westlaw search of "section /3 2 /3 sherman & product +1 market" (January 15, 2020), which yielded 73 hits for the past year and 186 hits for the past three years.
4. United States v. Microsoft Corp., 253 F.3d 34, 46 (D.C. Cir. 2001).
5. Based on a Westlaw search of "section /3 2 /3 sherman & labor +1 market" (January 15, 2020). This search, like the earlier ones, should be taken with many grains of salt because of variations in how judges write opinions and the types of issues that arise in these cases, but they give one a rough sense of litigation patterns.
6. 680 F.2d 1263,1265 (9th Cir. 1982).
7. *Id.* at 1267.
8. Brunswick Corp. v. Pueblo Bowl-O-Mat, Inc., 429 U.S. 477, 487–88 (1977).
9. *See* Thomsen v. Western Elec. Co., 660 F.2d at 1267.
10. 5 F. Supp. 2d 694, 698 (D. Minn. 1998), aff'd, 208 F.3d 655, 659 (8th Cir. 2000).
11. *Id.* at 701–3.
12. *Id.* at 706–7.
13. *See* U.S. Dept. of Labor, *Occupational Employment Statistics* (2016), available at https://www.bls.gov/oes/current/oes_stru.htm [https://perma.cc/E2FX-2V7E].
14. *See* Ioana Marinescu & Ronald Wolthoff, *Opening the Black Box of the Matching Function: The Power of Words*, NBER Working Paper No. 22508, 15 (2016).
15. Alexandre Mas & Amanda Pallais, *Valuing Alternative Work Arrangements*, 107 AM. ECON. REV. 3722 (2017).
16. José Azar, Ioana Marinescu & Marshall Steinbaum, *Measuring Labor Market Power Two Ways*, 109 AM. ECON. ASS'N PAPERS & PROC., 317 (2019).
17. ALAN MANNING, MONOPSONY IN MOTION: IMPERFECT COMPETITION IN LABOR MARKETS, at 1012 (2003).
18. Guido Matias Cortes & Giovanni Gallipoli, *The Costs of Occupational Mobility: An Aggregate Analysis*, 16 J. Eur. Econ. Ass'n 275, 312–13 (2018).
19. *Id.* at 279.
20. *Id.* at 302, table 7.
21. Erhan Artuç & John McLaren, *Trade Policy and Wage Inequality: A Structural Analysis with Occupational and Sectoral Mobility*, 97 J. INT'L ECON. 278, 284 (2015); Etienne Lalé, *Worker Reallocation across Occupations: Confronting Data with Theory*, 44 LAB. ECON. 51, 59 (2017)

(finding that mobility costs "fluctuate between 54 and 67% of annual earnings").

22. *See* U.S. Dep't of Agriculture, Commuting Zones and Labor Market Areas (2012), available at https://www.ers.usda.gov/data-products/ commuting-zones-and-labor-market-areas/ [https://perma.cc/ E2KR-2EZ2].

23. Efraim Benmelech, Nittai Bergman & Hyunseob Kim, *Strong Employers and Weak Employees: How Does Employer Concentration Affect Wages?,* NBER Working Paper No. 24037, at 13–14 (2018), https://www.nber.org/ papers/w24147.pdf; Kevin Rinz, *Labor Market Concentration, Earnings Inequality, and Earnings Mobility,* Center for Economic Studies, U.S. Census Bureau Working Paper 2018-10, 30 (2018); Brad Hershbein, Claudia Macaluso & Chen Yeh, *Concentration in U.S. Local Labor Markets: Evidence from Vacancy and Employment Data* at 12–13 (unpub., 2018); Yue Qiu & Aaron Sojourner, *Labor-Market Concentration and Labor Compensation* at 21–22 (unpub., 2019).

24. *See* Alan Manning & Barbara Petrongolo, *How Local Are Labor Markets? Evidence from a Spatial Job Search Model,* 107 Am. Econ. Rev. 2877 (2017).

25. *See, e.g.,* Reed v. Advocate Health Care, 268 F.R.D. 573, 590 (N.D. Ill. 2009).

26. U.S. Dep't of Justice & Federal Trade Comm'n, Horizontal Merger Guidelines (2010), at § 5.3.

27. *See* Azar et al., *supra* note 16. In this paper, the labor supply elasticity is approximated by the application elasticity, i.e., the percent increase in applications that results from a percent increase in the advertised wage.

28. *Id.*

29. *See* U.S. Dep't of Justice & Federal Trade Comm'n, *Horizontal Merger Guidelines,* § 4.1 (2010) (describing the rule for product markets); Suresh Naidu, Eric A. Posner & E. Glen Weyl, *Antitrust Remedies for Labor Market Power,* 132 Harv. L. Rev. 536, 574–75 (2018).

30. Azar et al., *supra* note 16, at 12.

31. *See* Brooke Grp. Ltd. v. Brown & Williamson Tobacco Corp., 509 U.S. 209, 226 (1993).

32. Aspen Skiing Co. v. Aspen Highlands Skiing Corp., 472 U.S. 585 (1985).

33. Danny Vinik, *The Real Future of Work,* Politico, Jan.–Feb. 2018, https:// www.politico.com/magazine/story/2018/01/04/future-work-independent- contractors-alternative-work-arrangements-216212.

34. David Weil, The Fissured Workplace: Why Work Became So Bad for So Many and What Can Be Done to Improve It (2014).

35. Microsoft Corp. v. United States, 373 F.3d 1199 (D.C. Cir. 2004).

36. For details of the proposal and a discussion, *see* Ionana Elena Marinescu & Eric A. Posner, *Why Has Antitrust Failed Workers?,* at 8–18 (Mar. 7, 2019), https://papers.ssrn.com/sol3/papers.cfm?abstract_id=3335174.

37. *See,* e.g., Colo. Interstate Gas Co. v. Natural Gas Pipeline Co. of Am., 885 F.2d 683, 694 n. 18 (10th Cir. 1989) ("[L]ower courts generally require a minimum market share of between 70% and 80%.").

38. 29 U.S.C. §§ 151–69 (2018). The Supreme Court expressed skepticism when a union brought an antitrust case against an employer who had tried to divert business to entities it controlled that were not unionized, allegedly to weaken the bargaining power of the union. The Court commented that this behavior "might constitute . . . an unfair labor practice . . . but in the context of the bargaining relationship between the parties to this litigation, such activities are plainly not subject to review under the federal antitrust laws." Associated Gen. Contractors of California, Inc. v. California State Council of Carpenters, 459 U.S. 519, 526–27 (1983). While the relationship between labor law and antitrust law is complex, I do not think antitrust claims should be ruled out when the alleged anticompetitive act is also an unfair labor practice.

39. For discussion, see chapter 6.

Chapter 5

1. 15 U.S.C. § 18.

2. Efraim Benmelech, Nittai Bergman & Hyunseob Kim, *Strong Employers and Weak Employees: How Does Employer Concentration Affect Wages?,* 4, NBER Working Paper No. 24307 (2018); Elena Prager & Matthew Schmitt, *Employer Consolidation and Wages: Evidence from Hospitals,* 4, Wash. Ctr. Equitable Growth (2019); David Arnold, *Mergers and Acquisitions, Local Labor Market Concentration, and Worker Outcomes* (unpub., 2019); Qi Ge, Donggeun Kim & Myongjin Kim, *Mergers and Labor Market Outcomes in the US Airline Industry* (unpub., 2020).

3. Statement of Commissioner Rohit Chopra, Federal Trade Commission, regarding Private Equity Roll-ups and the Hard-Scott-Rodino Annual Report to Congress, Commission File No. P110014, July 8, 2020.

4. Noam Scheiber & Ben Casselman, *Why Is Pay Lagging? Maybe Too Many Mergers in the Heartland,* New York Times, Jan. 25, 2018.

5. *Id.*

6. *Id.* at § 7.

7. Louis Kaplow has cogently made this argument in a series of articles. *See,* e.g., Louis Kaplow, *Market Definition: Impossible and Counterproductive,* 79 Antitrust L. J. 1 (2013).

8. See Joseph Farrell & Carl Shapiro, *Antitrust Evaluation of Horizontal Mergers: An Economic Alternative to Market Definition,* 10 B. E. J. Theoretical Econ (2010).

9. U.S. Dep't of Justice & Federal Trade Comm'n, *Horizontal Merger Guidelines* (2010).

10. E. Glen Weyl & Michael Fabinger, *Pass-Through as an Economic Tool: Principles of Incidence under Imperfect Competition,* 121 J. Pol. Econ.

528 (2013); Sonia Jaffe & E. Glen Weyl, *The First-Order Approach to Merger Analysis*, 5 AM. ECON. J.: MICROECONOMICS 188 (2013).

11. *See* Herbert Hovenkamp, *Appraising Merger Efficiencies*, 24 GEO. MASON L. REV. 703 (2017).

12. *Horizontal Merger Guidelines*, *supra* note 9, at § 10.

13. *See* F.T.C. v. Univ. Health, Inc., 938 F.2d 1206, 1223 (11th Cir. 1991); PHILLIP E. AREEDA & HERBERT HOVENKAMP, ANTITRUST LAW: AN ANALYSIS OF ANTITRUST PRINCIPLES AND THEIR APPLICATION ¶ 971, at 41 (2016) (efficiencies generated by the merger must be passed on to the consumer to a sufficient extent that, despite anticompetitive effects, "the post-merger price is no higher than the pre-merger price").

14. Mark Armstrong & John Vickers, *A Model of Delegated Project Choice*, 78 ECONOMETRICA 213 (2010).

15. *Horizontal Merger Guidelines*, supra note 9, at § 10.

16. Clayton J. Masterman, Note, *The Customer Is Not Always Right: Balancing Worker and Customer Welfare in Antitrust Law*, 69 VAND. L. REV. 1387 (2016), at 1416. *See* C. Scott Hemphill & Nancy L. Rose, *Mergers That Harm Sellers*, 127 YALE L. J. 2078, 2087–92 (2018) for a defense of this view, which they more broadly call the "trading partner welfare standard."

17. However, empirical evidence verifies that workers who are laid off suffer significant harms and have trouble finding equally good jobs. *See,* e.g., Steven J. Davis & Till von Wachter, *Recessions and the Costs of Job Loss*, 2 BROOKINGS PAPERS ON ECONOMIC ACTIVITY (2011); Johannes F. Schmieder, Till von Wachter & Joerg Heining, *The Costs of Job Displacement over the Business Cycle and Its Sources: Evidence from Germany* (unpub., 2018).

18.   Areeda & Hovenkamp, *supra* note 13, ¶ 971, at 41.

19. *See,* e.g., Géarard Gaudet & Ngo Van Long, *Vertical Integration, Foreclosure, and Profits in the Presence of Double Marginalization*, 5 J. ECON. & MAN. STRATEGY 409 (1996).

20. Gregory S. Crawford, Robin S. Lee, Michael D. Whinston & Ali Yurukoglu, *The Welfare Effects of Vertical Integration in Multichannel Television Markets,* NBER Working Paper No. 21832 (2017).

21. *See* Joseph Farrell and Michael K. Katz, *The Economics of Welfare Standards in Antitrust*, 2 COMPETITION POLICY INTERNATIONAL 3 (2006).

22. The analysis in the appendix is drawn from Suresh Naidu, Eric A. Posner & Glen Weyl, *Antitrust Remedies for Labor Market Power*, 132 HARV. L. REV. 536 (2018), where further details are supplied.

23. The pre-merger HHI is $3 * 1/3^2 = 0.3333$. The post-merger HHI is $2/3^2 + 1/3^2 = 0.5556$.

24. Barry T. Hirsch & Edward J. Schumacher, *Classic or New Monopsony? Searching for Evidence in Nursing Labor Markets*, 24 J. HEALTH ECON. 969 (2005).

25. José Azar, Ioana Marinescu & Marshall Steinbaum, *Labor Market Concentration*, NBER Working Paper No. 24147 (2019).

26. Bureau of Labor Statistics, Registered Nurses Median Pay (2016), https://www.bls.gov/ooh/healthcare/registered-nurses.htm.

27. *See* Douglas O. Staiger, Joanne Spetz & Ciaran S. Phibbs, *Is There Monopsony in the Labor Market? Evidence from a Natural Experiment*, 28 J. Lab. Econ. 211 (2010).

28. For further details, *see* Naidu et al., *supra* note 22.

Chapter 6

1. Dave Jamieson, *Jimmy John's Makes Low-Wage Workers Sign "Oppressive" Noncompete Agreements*, HuffPost, Oct. 13, 2014, https://www.huffingtonpost.com/2014/10/13/jimmy-johns-non-compete_n_5978180.html.

2. *See,* e.g., Press release, Office of the Attorney General for the State of Illinois, *Madigan Announces Settlement with Jimmy John's for Imposing Unlawful Non-Compete Agreements*, Dec. 7, 2016, www.illinoisattorneygeneral.gov/pressroom/2016_12/20161207.html; Press release, Office of the Attorney General for the State of New York, *A. G. Schneiderman Announces Settlement with Jimmy John's to Stop Including Non-Compete Agreements in Hiring Packets*, June 22, 2016, www.ag.ny.gov/press-release/2016/ag-schneiderman-announces-settlement-jimmy-johns-stop-including-non-compete.

3. My focus is on "employee noncompetes." I do not address the use of noncompetes in other settings, for example, as part of the sale of a business. I also exclude franchise no-poaching clauses from the general discussion.

4. *See* Evan Starr, J. J. Prescott & Norman Bishara, *Noncompetes in the U.S. Labor Force,* 1–4, U. Mich. L. & Econ. Research Paper No. 18-013 (2019). The authors found that 18.1% of the U.S. labor force, or roughly 28 million people, were subject to a noncompete agreement as of 2014, and nearly 40% have signed a noncompete at some point in their careers. *Id.* at 2.

5. *See id.* at 16–17. Approximately 14.3% of workers without a bachelor's degree were subject to noncompetes in 2014, compared to 26.6% of those with bachelor's degrees. *Id.*

6. Harlan M. Blake, *Employee Agreements Not to Compete,* 73 Harv. L. Rev. 625, 633–34 (1960).

7. Y.B. 2 Hen. 5, fn. 5, pl. 26 (1414). *See also* Blake, *supra,* note 6, at 631–32.

8. *See* Blake, *supra* note 6, at 634–37.

9. *Id.*; *see also* Cathy Packer & Johanna Cleary, *Rediscovering the Public Interest: An Analysis of the Common Law Governing Post-Employment Non-Compete Contracts for Media Employees,* 24 Cardozo Arts & Ent. L.J.

1073, 1078–82 (2007); *Act for Avoiding of Exactions Taken upon Apprentices*, 28 Hen. 8, Ch. 5 (1536).

10. 1 P. Wms. 181, 24 Eng. Rep. 347 (Q.B. 1711). For a discussion of the case and its influence, *see* Blake, *supra* note 6, at 629–46.

11. *See* Blake, *supra* note 6, at 653; Jordan Leibman & Richard Nathan, *The Enforceability of Post-Employment Noncompetition Agreements Formed after At-Will Employment Has Commenced: The "Afterthought" Agreement*, 60 S. CAL. L. REV. 1465, 1484 (1987).

12. *See, e.g.*, Curtis 1000, Inc. v. Suess, 24 F.3d 941, 947 (7th Cir. 1994).

13. 40 N.Y.2d 303 (N.Y. App. Div. 1976).

14. 674 F. Supp. 1039 (S.D.N.Y. 1987).

15. In addition to examining whether the noncompete is sufficiently tailored to the protectable interest at stake, courts often examine two additional factors: (1) whether the agreement is "injurious to the public" and (2) whether, on balance, the agreement imposes excessive hardship on the employee. *See* Kenneth R. Swift, *Void Agreements, Knocked-Out Terms, and Blue Pencils: Judicial and Legislative Handling of Unreasonable Terms in Noncompete Agreements*, 24 HOFSTRA LAB. & EMP. L.J. 223, 231–32 n.37 (2007) (listing cases).

16. *See* Valley Med. Specialists v. Farber, 194 Ariz. 363, 370 (1999) (en banc).

17. *See, e.g.*, McCann Surveyors, Inc. v. Evans, 611 A.2d 1, 3–4 (Del. Ch. 1987).

18. Curtis 1000, Inc. v. Suess, 24 F.3d 941, 947 (7th Cir. 1994).

19. *See, e.g.*, Vantage Tech. L.L.C. v. Cross, 17 S.W.3d 637, 645 (Tenn. Ct. App. 1999).

20. Harvey J. Goldschmid, *Antitrust's Neglected Stepchild: A Proposal for Dealing with Restrictive Covenants under Federal Law*, 73 COLUM. L. REV. 1173, 1204–6 (1973).

21. *Id.* at 1206.

22. Miller v. Kimberly-Clark Corp., 339 F. Supp. 1296, 1298 (E.D. Wis. 1971) (dismissing antitrust challenge because the noncompete was not a "public" injury); Alders v. AFA Corp. of Fla., 353 F. Supp. 654 (S.D. Fla. 1973), *aff'd*, 490 F.2d 990 (5th Cir. 1974) (dismissing antitrust challenge because noncompete was reasonable).

23. The search term was "sherman +1 act & (noncompete covenant +4 compete)," which yielded 17 hits over the past three years (search from Jan. 1, 2017 to Jan. 1, 2020), and 55 hits over the past 10 years (search from Jan. 1, 2010 to Jan. 1, 2020). Many of these cases do involve not employment noncompetes but noncompetes that are ancillary to the sales of businesses. The one (ambiguous) exception is the *Renown Health* case brought by the FTC in which merging firms agreed to drop noncompetes in order to maintain competition in the market for cardiologists. Renown Health, FTC Docket No. C-4366, FTC File No. 1110101 (Nov. 30,

2012) (Decision and Order), www.ftc.gov/sites/default/files/documents/cases/2012/12/121204renownhealthdo.pdf.

24. Paul H. Rubin & Peter Shedd, *Human Capital and Covenants Not to Compete*, 10 J. LEGAL STUD. 93 (1981).

25. GARY S. BECKER, HUMAN CAPITAL (3d ed. 1993) (1964).

26. *See, e.g.,* Rubin & Shedd, *supra* note 24, at 96; Daron Acemoglu & Jörn-Steffen Pischke, *Why Do Firms Train? Theory and Evidence*, 113 Q. J. ECON. 79, 80, 113 (1998).

27. *See* Daron Acemoglu & Jörn-Steffen Pischke, *Certification of Training and Training Outcomes*, 44 EUR. ECON. REV. 917, 918 (2000).

28. *See* Christopher D. Hampson, *The New American Debtors' Prisons*, 44 AM. J. CRIM. L. 1, 22–24 (2016). By the 1870s, nearly every state had abolished or discontinued the debtors' prison. *Id.* at 19.

29. A Westlaw search for references to the article yielded eight cases. *See, e.g.,* Curtis 1000, Inc. v. Suess, 24 F.3d 941, 947 (7th Cir. 1994) (citing Rubin & Shedd for the proposition that noncompetes can be used as devices to protect investment in human capital); Kenyon Int'l Emergency Servs., Inc. v. Malcolm, No. H-09-3550, 2010 WL 452745, at *3 (S.D. Tex. Feb. 8, 2010) ("Covenants not to compete encourage business growth by protecting the employer's investment in human capital.").

30. *See* Jessica S. Jeffers, *The Impact of Restricting Labor Mobility on Corporate Investment and Entrepreneurship* 26–28 (unpub., Dec. 24, 2019), https://papers.ssrn.com/sol3/papers.cfm?abstract_id=3040393.

31. "Customer relationship" is a term of art in many states, but the analysis holds for relationships with suppliers, investors, and other stakeholders.

32. *See, e.g.,* Daron Acemoglu & Jörn-Steffen Pischke, *The Structure of Wages and Investment in General Training*, 107 J. POL. ECON. 539, 540 (1999); Acemoglu & Pischke, *supra* note 26, at 80; Daron Acemoglu & Jörn-Steffen Pischke, *Beyond Becker: Training in Imperfect Labour Markets*, 109 ECON. J. 112 (2001).

33. Acemoglu & Pischke, *supra* note 26, at 80.

34. As one judge flatly stated, "If covenants not to compete are forbidden, the employer will pay a lower wage." Outsource Int'l, Inc. v. Barton, 192 F.3d 662, 670 (7th Cir. 1999) (dissent).

35. Mark J. Garmaise, *Ties That Truly Bind: Noncompetition Agreements, Executive Compensation, and Firm Investment*, 27 J. L. ECON. & ORG. 376 (2011).

36. Jeffers, *supra* note 30, at 5. Unlike Garmaise, Jeffers did not find a statistically significant change (negative or positive) in the investment-to-labor ratio. *Id.* at 5 n.3.

37. Evan Starr, *Consider This: Training, Wages and the Enforceability of Covenants Not to Compete*, 72 INDUS. & LABOR REL. REV. 783, 785 (2019).

38. *See* Raffaele Conti, *Do Non-Competition Agreements Lead Firms to Pursue Risky R&D Projects?*, 35 STRAT. MGMT. J. 1230, 1230–31, 1243

(2014) (finding that noncompete enforcement mitigates firm concerns about knowledge leakages, permitting the firm to pursue riskier R&D projects); Kurt Lavetti, Carol J. Simon & William D. White, *Buying Loyalty: Theory and Evidence from Physicians* 29 (unpub., Feb. 1, 2014), https://papers.ssrn.com/sol3/papers.cfm?abstract_id=2439068 (finding that physicians subject to noncompetes earn higher wages and receive greater returns to tenure and experience, consistent with higher levels of investment).

39. *See* Outsource Int'l, Inc. v. Barton, 192 F.3d 662, 670 (7th Cir. 1999) (dissent); Mark A. Glick et al., *The Law and Economics of Post-Employment Covenants: A Unified Framework*, 11 GEO. MASON L. REV. 357, 417–18 (2002); Rubin & Shedd, *supra* note 24, at 100–102.

40. *See* W. KIP VISCUSI, PRICING LIVES: GUIDEPOSTS FOR A SAFER SOCIETY (2018) (providing a recent discussion).

41. *See* Starr et al., *supra* note 4, at 20 (finding that over 30% of workers were asked to sign a noncompete *after* accepting an employment offer and that fewer than 10% of workers negotiate over their noncompetes); *see also* Matt Marx, *The Firm Strikes Back: Non-Compete Agreements and the Mobility of Technical Professionals*, 76 AM. SOC. REV. 695, 706 (2011) (finding that 70% of engineers in sample received their noncompetes *after* signing their employment contracts).

42. In the optimal contracts literature, a similar point was made about liquidated damages clauses. *See* Philippe Aghion & Patrick Bolton, *Contracts as a Barrier to Entry*, 77 AM. ECON. REV. 388 (1987); Tai-Yeong Chung, *On the Social Optimality of Liquidated Damages Clauses: An Economic Analysis*, 8 J. L. ECON. & ORG. 280 (1992). The argument was further developed for covenants not to compete in Eric A. Posner, Alexander J. Triantis & George G. Triantis, *Investing in Human Capital: The Efficiency of Covenants Not to Compete*, Univ. of Va. L. Sch. John M. Olin Program in L. & Econ. Working Paper Series No. 11 (2004).

43. *See generally* Steven C. Salop, *Anticompetitive Overbuying by Power Buyers*, 72 ANTITRUST L. J. 669, 675–82 (2005).

44. Some noncompetes forbid employees to *prepare* to compete and thus to make such agreements while still employed by the incumbent employer. *See*, e.g., Stork H. & E. Turbo Blading, Inc. v. Berry, 32 Misc. 3d 1208(A), 932 N.Y.S.2d 763 (N.Y. Sup. Ct. 2011). These noncompetes would be even more effective at blocking entry than ordinary noncompetes.

45. The argument goes back to Aghion & Bolton, *supra* note 42; Eric B. Rasmusen, Mark J. Ramseyer & John S. Wiley Jr., *Naked Exclusion*, 81 AM. ECON. REV. 1137 (1991).

46. Starr, *supra* note 37, at 799.

47. Natarajan Balasubramanian et al., *Locked In? The Enforceability of Covenants Not to Compete and the Careers of High-Tech Workers*, 4, U.S.

Census Bureau Ctr. for Econ. Studies Paper No. CES-WP-17-09 (2019), https://papers.ssrn.com/sol3/papers.cfm?abstract_id=2905782.

48. Garmaise, *supra* note 35 at 402. *See also* Norman Bishara, Kenneth J. Martin & Randall S. Thomas, *An Empirical Analysis of Noncompetition Clauses and Other Restrictive Postemployment Covenants*, 68 VAND. L. REV. 1, 3–5 (2015) (finding that 80% of CEO contracts contain a noncompete term and presenting empirical data about the terms of these contracts).

49. Michael Lipsitz & Evan Starr, *Low-Wage Workers and the Enforceability of Non-Compete Agreements* (unpub., Dec. 9, 2019), https://papers.ssrn.com/sol3/papers.cfm?abstract_id=3452240.

50. Matthew S. Johnson, Kurt Lavetti & Michael Lipsitz, *The Labor Effects of Legal Restrictions on Worker Mobility* 2 (unpub., Sept. 22, 2019), https://papers.ssrn.com/sol3/papers.cfm?abstract_id=3455381.

51. Evan Starr, Natarajan Balasubramanian & Mariko Sakakibara, *Screening Spinouts? How Noncompete Enforceability Affects the Creation, Growth, and Survival of New Firms*, 64 MGMT. SCI. 552, 552–53 (2018).

52. *Id.* at 567.

53. Jeffers, *supra* note 30, at 3. *See also* Robert C. Bird & John D. Knopf, *The Impact of Local Knowledge on Banking*, 48 J. FIN. SERVS. RES. 1, 3 (2015) (finding similar negative effects on the entry of new banks).

54. Sampsa Samila & Olav Sorenson, *Noncompete Covenants: Incentives to Innovate or Impediments to Growth*, 57 MGMT. SCI. 425, 426 (2011).

55. Hyo Kang & Lee Fleming, *Non-competes, Business Dynamism, and Concentration: Evidence from a Florida Case Study*, 2, Searle Center Working Paper Series 2017-046 (2019).

56. Evan Starr, *The Use, Abuse, and Enforceability of Non-Compete and No-Poach Agreements: A Brief Review of the Theory, Evidence, and Recent Reform Efforts*, ECON. INNOVATION GRP. 12 (Feb. 20, 2019), www.eig.org/wp-content/uploads/2019/02/Non-Competes-2.20.19.pdf.

57. *See* Starr et al., *supra* note 51; Bruce Fallick, Charles A. Fleischman & James B. Rebitzer, *Job-Hopping in Silicon Valley: Some Evidence concerning the Micro-Foundations of a High Technology Cluster*, 88 REV. ECON. & STATS. 472 (2006); Jeffers, *supra* note 30, at 3; Johnson et al., *supra* note 50; Lipsitz & Starr, *supra* note 49; Matt Marx, Jasjit Singh & Lee Fleming, *Regional Disadvantage? Employee Non-Compete Agreements and Brain Drain*, 44 RES. POL'Y 394, 403 (2015); Matt Marx, Deborah Strumsky & Lee Fleming, *Mobility, Skills, and the Michigan Non-Compete Experiment*, 55 MGMT. SCI. 875, 876 (2009) (discussing inventors in Michigan); Starr, *supra* note 37, at 798.

58. *See* J. J. Prescott & Evan Starr, *Subject Beliefs about Contract Enforceability* (unpub., 2019) (on file with author) (finding that workers believe noncompetes are generally enforceable, even when they are not, and that firms in nonenforcing states appear to try to keep their workers misinformed about the law); Starr et al., *supra* note 4, at 32 (noting that

noncompete agreements appear frequently, even in states that limit their enforceability).

59. Raven Molloy et al., *Understanding Declining Fluidity in the U.S. Labor Market*, 47 BROOKINGS INST. 183, 185 (2016),www.brookings.edu/wp-content/uploads/2016/03/molloytextspring16bpea.pdf (noting that labor market fluidity has declined by 10% to 15% since the 1980s).

60. Rubin & Shedd, *supra* note 24, at 100.

61. Starr et al., *supra* note 4, at 16–17.

62. *Id.*

63. Alexander J. S. Colvin & Heidi Shierholz, *Noncompete Agreements: Ubiquitous, Harmful to Wages and to Competition, and Part of a Growing Trend of Employers Requiring Workers to Sign Away Their Rights*, ECON. POL'Y INST. (2019), www.epi.org/files/pdf/179414.pdf.

64. *See, e.g.,* United States v. Topco Assocs., 405 U.S. 596, 606 (1972).

65. *See, e.g.,* Lektro-Vend Corp. v. Vendo Co., 660 F.2d 255, 265 (1981).

66. For a discussion, *see* Mark S. Popofsky, *Defining Exclusionary Conduct: Section 2, The Rule of Reason, and the Unifying Principle Underlying Antitrust Rules*, 73 ANTITRUST L. J. 435 (2006).

67. Bus. Elecs. Corp. v. Sharp Elecs. Corp., 480 U.S. 717, 729 n.3 (1988).

68. For a helpful discussion, *see* Edward D. Cavanaugh, *Whatever Happened to Quick Look?*, 26 U. MIAMI BUS. L. REV. 39 (2017).

69. The Antitrust Division has taken the position that a naked, horizontal agreement not to poach a competitor's employees is per se unlawful. *See* Statement of Interest of the United States, *In re: Railway Industry Employee No-Poach Antitrust Litig.*, 2:18-mc-00798 (W.D. Pa. Feb. 8, 2019).

Chapter 7

1. Efraim Benmelech, Nittai Bergman & Hyunseob Kim, *Strong Employers and Weak Employees: How Does Employer Concentration Affect Wages?*, NBER Working Paper No. 24307 (2018), https://www.nber.org/papers/w24307.

2. Or international but American antitrust law focuses on national effects.

3. On the matching problem in labor markets, *see* Sydnee Caldwell & Oren Danieli, *Outside Options in the Labor Market* (Nov. 7, 2018), http://scholar.harvard.edu/files/danieli/files/danieli_jmp.pdf.

4. Suresh Naidu & Eric A. Posner, *Labor Monopsony and the Limits of the Law* (Jan. 31, 2019), http://papers.ssrn.com/sol3/papers.cfm?abstract_id=3365374.

Chapter 8

1. The literature is too vast to cite. A recent contribution is Doruk Cengiz, Arindrajit Dube, Attila Lindner & Ben Zipperer, *The Effect of Minimum Wages on Low-Wage Jobs*, 134 Q. J. ECON. 1405 (2019).

2. Thomas Macurdy, *How Effective Is the Minimum Wage at Supporting the Poor?*, 123 J. Pol. Econ. 497 (2015); Peter Harasztosi & Attila Lindner, *Who Pays for the Minimum Wage?*, 109 Amer. Econ. Rev. 2693 (2019).

3. David Madland, *Wage Boards for American Workers*, Center for American Progress (Apr. 9, 2019).

4. Recent evidence on the EITC in Henrik Kleven, *The EITC and the Extensive Margin: A Reappraisal*, NBER Working Paper No. 26405 (2019), https://www.nber.org/papers/w26405.pdf has put in flux the literature, as in Hilary Hoynes & Jesse Rothstein, *Tax Policy toward Low-Income Families*, NBER Working Paper No. 22080 (2016), https://www.nber.org/papers/w22080.pdf, as it is no longer clear that the EITC significantly increases labor force participation among affected people.

5. Simon Jäger, Benjamin Schoefer, Samuel G. Young & Josef Zweimüller, *Wages and the Value of Nonemployment* (unpub., Feb. 9, 2020), https://papers.ssrn.com/sol3/papers.cfm?abstract_id=3520196.

6. Similar arguments about raising the value of unemployment as a device to reduce monopsony power (e.g., via a Universal Basic Income or wealth redistribution) could be made: David Card, Ana Rute Cardoso, Joerg Heining & Patrick Kline, *Firms and Labor Market Inequality: Evidence and Some Theory*, 36 J. Lab. Econ. 13 (2018) model the residual supply elasticity is increasing in the difference between the outside option and the wage; as this goes to zero, the degree of monopsony power likewise goes to zero.

7. Employment Law Handbook, *Illinois Employment and Labor Laws* (last visited July 30, 2020), https://www.dol.gov/general/aboutdol/majorlaws.

8. U.S. Department of Labor, *Summary of the Major Laws of the Department of Labor* (last visited July 30, 2020), https://www.employmentlawhandbook.com/state-employment-and-labor-laws/illinois/.

9. Lawrence H. Summers, *Some Simple Economics of Mandated Benefits*, 79 Am. Econ. Rev. 177 (1989).

10. Michael A. Spence, *Monopoly, Quality, and Regulation*, 6 Bell J. Econ 417 (1975).

11. Note that this implies that the usual practice in cost-benefit analysis of analyzing wage differentials across risky professions to assess the price of risks is suspect: monopsony implies that this empirical relationship traces out the valuation only for the marginal worker, not the average worker.

12. Summers, *supra* note 9 at 179 n.2.

13. *See* Summers, *supra* note 9.

14. This is analogous to the problem of "too many varieties" vs. "too few varieties," both of which are possible in monopolistically competitive markets as in, e.g., Avinash K. Dixit & Joseph E. Stiglitz, *Monopolistic Competition and Optimum Product Diversity*, 67 Am. Econ. Rev. 297 (1977).

15. RICHARD B. FREEMAN & JAMES L. MEDOFF, WHAT DO UNIONS DO? (1984).

16. Henry Farber & Daniel Saks, *Why Workers Want Unions: The Role of Relative Wages and Job Characteristics*, 88 J. POL. ECON. 349 (1980).

17. *See* Efraim Benmelech, Nittai Bergman & Hyunseob Kim, *Strong Employers and Weak Employees: How Does Employer Concentration Affect Wages?*, 4, NBER Working Paper No. 24307 (2018); Elena Prager & Matthew Schmitt, *Employer Consolidation and Wages: Evidence from Hospitals*, 4, Wash. Ctr. Equitable Growth (2019).

18. Brigham Frandsen, *The Surprising Impacts of Unionization on Establishments: Accounting for Selection in Close Union Representation Elections* (unpub., 2013) (on file with the Department of Economics, Brigham Young University).

19. John Schmitt & Ben Zipperer, *Dropping the Ax: Illegal Firings during Union Election Campaigns, 1951–2007*, EPRN, 2009, http://www.lerachapters.org/OJS/ojs-2.4.4-1/index.php/EPRN/article/viewFile/1875/1873.

20. *See* Benjamin Ward, *The Firm in Illyria: Market Syndicalism*, 48 AM. ECON REV. 566 (1958); *see also* GREGORY DOW, GOVERNING THE FIRM (2003).

21. Douglas Kruse, *Does Employee Ownership Improve Performance?*, IZA WORLD OF LABOR (2016), https://wol.iza.org/articles/does-employee-ownership-improve-performance/long.

Chapter 9

1. Some commentators claim that these alternative work arrangements (outside the employment relationship) have transformed labor markets throughout the United States, a claim that received a boost from a 2016 study that found alternative work arrangements increased from 10.7% in 2005 to 15.8% in 2015. *See* Lawrence F. Katz & Alan B. Krueger, *The Rise and Nature of Alternative Work Arrangements in the United States, 1995–2015*, NBER Working Paper No. 22667 (2016), https://www.nber.org/papers/w22667. However, the authors later revised their estimate down to a 1% increase. *See* Lawrence F. Katz % Alan B. Krueger, *Understanding Trends in Alternative Work Arrangements in the United States*, NBER Working Paper No. 25425 (2016), https://www.nber.org/papers/w25425.

2. *See, e.g.*, Keith Cunningham-Parmeter, *From Amazon to Uber: Defining Employment in the Modern Economy*, 96 B.U. L. REV. 1673, 1677 (2016); Brishen Rogers, *Employment Rights in the Platform Economy: Getting Back to Basics*, 10 HARV. L. & POL'Y REV. 479, 500, 505–7 (2016); Jennifer Pinsof, Note, *A New Take on an Old Problem: Employee Misclassification in the Modern Gig-Economy*, 22 MICH. TELECOMM. & TECH. L. REV. 341, 344 (2016); Seth D. Harris & Alan Krueger, *A Proposal for Modernizing Labor Laws for Twenty-First-Century Work: The "Independent Worker,"* Brookings Inst. (2015).

3. *See* John A. Pearce II & Jonathan P. Silva, *The Future of Independent Contractors and Their Status as Non-Employees: Moving on from a Common Law Standard*, 14 HASTINGS BUS. L. J. 1, 3 (2018); Alexia Fernández Campbell, *Companies Often Mislabel Employees as "Freelancers" to Cut Costs: Workers Are Fighting Back*, Vox, Mar. 20, 2019, https://www.vox.com/policy-and-politics/2019/3/20/18272918/conde-nast-epicurious-employee-freelancer-contractor; Harris & Krueger (Brookings Institute Discussion Paper 2015–10, 2015), *supra* note 2, at 7. Allegations of misclassification have led to a flurry of class action lawsuits. *See* Liya Palagashvili, *Disrupting the Employee and Contractor Laws*, 2017 U. CHI. LEGAL F. 379, 382–83, 405–8 (2017).

4. Preetika Rana, *Uber Tests Feature Allowing Some California Drivers to Set Fares*, WALL ST. J., Jan. 21, 2020, https://www.wsj.com/articles/uber-is-testing-a-feature-that-lets-some-california-drivers-set-fares-11579600801.

5. Ronald H. Coase, *The Nature of the Firm*, 4 ECONOMICA 386, 403–4 (1937).

6. *See* Scott E. Masten, *Legal Basis for the Firm*, 4 J. LAW, ECON. & ORG. 181 (1988).

7. Armen A. Alchian & Harold Demsetz, *Production, Information Costs, and Economic Organization*, 62 AMER. ECON. REV. 777, 778 (1972).

8. The starting point for this literature is a series of articles by Sanford Grossman, Oliver Hart, and John Moore, who pointed out that because contracts are necessarily incomplete (in the sense of being unable to specify all the optimal actions for both parties), it is important for the parties to specify which party will have discretion within the scope of incompleteness. The parties can assign discretion by allocating property rights: the party with a relevant property right has discretion over the use of that property—"residual" discretion or control in the sense that the discretion is limited by any specified contractual terms. The parties should then assign that discretion (via the assignment of property rights) to whichever party is more likely to use discretion in the joint interest of both parties—and that is roughly the party whose incentive to invest in the joint project is more sensitive to the return on that investment. The difference between an employee and a contractor is that the employee does not own the asset in which she applies her labor—that asset is owned by the employer—while a contractor does own the asset. The contractor has greater bargaining power vis-à-vis the firm and stronger incentive to maintain the asset but a weaker incentive to use the asset to benefit the firm. *See generally* Sanford J. Grossman & Oliver D. Hart, *The Costs and Benefits of Ownership: A Theory of Vertical and Lateral Integration*, 94 J. POLIT. ECON. 691 (1986); Oliver Hart & John Moore, *Property Rights and the Nature of the Firm*, 98 J. POLIT. ECON. 1119 (1990); Philippe Aghion and Richard Holden provide a lucid discussion. *See* Philippe Aghion & Richard Holden, *Incomplete Contracts and the Theory of the Firm: What*

Have We Learned over the Past 25 Years?, 25 J. ECON. PERSPECTIVES 181 (2011). Other authors further developed the special role of the employee. *See*, e.g., Bengt Holmstrom & John Roberts, *The Boundaries of the Firm Revisited*, 12 J. ECON. PERSPECTIVES 73 (1998); George P. Baker & Thomas N. Hubbard, *Make versus Buy in Trucking: Asset Ownership, Job Design, and Information*, 93 AMER. ECON. REV. 551 (2003); Eric Van den Steen, *On the Origin of Shared Beliefs (and Corporate Culture)*, 41 RAND J. ECON. 617 (2010); Wouter Dessein, *Incomplete Contracts and Firm Boundaries*, 30 J. L., ECON., & ORG. (2014). For an early piece that anticipated some of these arguments, *see* Alchian & Demsetz, *supra* note 7, at 778, who argue that firms need control over employees because of the difficulty of controlling team production by contract.

9. George P. Baker & Thomas N. Hubbard, *Contractibility and Asset Ownership: On-Board Computers and Governance in U.S. Trucking*, 1443 QUARTERLY J. ECON. 1443, 1443 (2004).

10. *Id.* at 1446.

11. *Id.* at 1447.

12. *Id.* at 1476.

13. *See* GARY S. BECKER, HUMAN CAPITAL (3d. ed., 1993).

14. *See* Richard R. Carlson, *Employment by Design: Employees, Independent Contractors and the Theory of the Firm*, 71 ARK. L. REV. 127, 146–47 (2018).

15. For a detailed illustration based on the Winchester Company, *see* John Buttrick, *The Inside Contract System*, 12 J. ECON. HIST. 205 (1952), and the very helpful discussion in Carlson, *supra* note 14 at 148–59. Buttrick observes that the "employees," more than the contractors, were subject to monopsony (because the employees ended up working exclusively for Winchester while the contractors sold their services to other companies as well), as does Carlson—my point here. But neither of them recognizes its centrality to the distinction between employer and contractor.

16. Two earlier law review papers draw on the theory of the firm, as I do, but offer different tests and do not derive the distinction between contractor and employee from the problem of labor market monopsony. *See* Matthew T. Bodie, *Participating as a Theory of Employment*, 89 NOTRE DAME L. REV. 661, 665–66 (2013) (arguing that an employee is a worker who "participates" in a firm); Carlson, *supra* note 14, at 130 (proposing a test that draws on employer's economic motives for hiring rather than buying labor).

17. If contractors require legal protection or other policy responses, the reasons lie elsewhere. For example, one might favor the extension of antidiscrimination norms in employment law to contractors because she believes that discrimination against contractors is morally reprehensible or that such an extension will advance public values. These arguments lie outside the narrow economic perspective that I take in this chapter.

18. For a discussion, *see* Suresh Naidu & Eric A. Posner, *Labor Monopsony and the Limits of the Law* (Jan. 31, 2019), http://papers.ssrn.com/sol3/papers.cfm?abstract_id=3365374. In the legal literature, Richard Epstein has used this insight to launch a wholesale assault on labor and employment law. *See,* e.g., RICHARD A. EPSTEIN, FORBIDDEN GROUNDS: THE CASE AGAINST EMPLOYMENT DISCRIMINATION LAWS (1992); Richard A. Epstein, *Contractual Solutions for Employment Law Problems*, 38 HARV. J. L. & PUB. POL'Y 789 (2015); Richard A. Epstein, *Labor Unions: Saviors or Scourges?*, 41 CAP. U. L. REV. 1 (2013). His argument is, of course, based on the assumption that labor markets are competitive, or nearly so.

19. For a recent overview of the empirical literature on labor market concentration, *see* Suresh Naidu, Eric A. Posner & Glen Weyl, *Antitrust Remedies for Labor Market Power*, 132 HARV. L. REV. 536, 560–69 (2018).

20. *See* Arindrajit Dube, T. William Lester & Michael Reich, *Minimum Wage Shocks, Employment Flows, and Labor Market Frictions*, 34 J. LAB. ECON. 663, 664 (2016); José Azar et al., *Minimum Wage Employment Effects and Labor Market Concentration*, 3–4, NBER Working Paper No. 26101 (2019). However, other scholars continue to disagree. For a discussion, *see* Katharine G. Abraham & Melissa S. Kearney, *Explaining the Decline in the US Employment-to-Population Ratio: A Review of the Evidence*, 59 J. ECON. LIT. 585, 624–27 (2020).

21. However, not all elements of employment law can be justified from a labor monopsony standpoint. When workers are paid above the minimum wage because of market competition, employment mandates and related protections do not benefit them and may harm them. *See* chapter 8.

22. Unless labor buyers violate the antitrust laws.

23. Indeed, even minimum wage laws may not help the poor. The reason is that they are very crude rules that can end up raising wages above the competitive rate even when labor monopsony exists; when they do, the higher costs may be passed on to low-income buyers. For empirical analysis, *see* Thomas Macurdy, *How Effective Is the Minimum Wage at Supporting the Poor?*, 123 J. POL. ECON. 497 (2015); Doruk Cengiz, Arindrajit Dube, Attila Lindner & Ben Zipperer, *The Effect of Minimum Wages on Low-Wage Jobs*, 134 Q. J. ECON. 1405 (2019).

24. For a statement of the common law test, *see* Cmty. for Creative Non-Violence v. Reid, 490 U.S. 730, 751–52 (1989).

25. Carlson, *supra* note 14, at 159–60. I discuss *respondeat superior* in § 9.5.

26. *See,* e.g., Bartels v. Birmingham, 332 U.S. 126, 130 (1947).

27. The factors are quoted from Scantland v. Jeffry Knight, Inc., 721 F.3d 1308, 1312 (11th Cir. 2013).

28. The Supreme Court recognized the difficulty of applying multifactor employment tests over 70 years ago. *See* NLRB v. Hearst Publications,

Inc., 322 U.S. 111, 121 (1944) ("Few problems in the law have given greater
variety of application and conflict in results than the cases arising in the
borderland between what is clearly an employer-employee relationship
and what is clearly one of independent entrepreneurial dealing."). *See also*
Carlson, *supra* note 14, at 171–74.

29. Assem. Bill 5, 2019–2020 Reg. Sess. (Cal. 2019), http://leginfo.legislature.
ca.gov/faces/billNavClient.xhtml?bill_id=201920200AB5.

30. *See* Joshua D. Angrist, Sydnee Caldwell & Jonathan V. Hall, *Uber vs.
Taxi: A Driver's Eye View,* 1–2, NBER Working Paper No. 23891 (2017),
https://www.nber.org/papers/w23891.pdf.

31. *See* Meyer v Kalanick, 174 F. Supp. 3d 817, 819–20 (S.D.N.Y. 2016),
vacated, Meyer v. Uber Technologies, Inc., 868 F.3d 66 (2d Cir. 2017).

32. *See* United States v. Hutcheson, 312 U.S. 219, 232, 235–37 (1941) (holding
that the Clayton Act and Norris-LaGuardia Act together provide unions a
statutory exemption from antitrust liability).

33. *See* Columbia River Packers Ass'n v. Hinton, 315 U.S. 143, 144–45 (1942)
(excluding "independent entrepreneurs" from the labor exception); L.A.
Meat and Provision Drivers Union, Local 626 v. United States, 371 U.S.
94, 96, 99–102 (1962) (same).

Conclusion

1. *See* DAVID WEIL, THE FISSURED WORKPLACE: WHY WORK BECAME SO
BAD FOR SO MANY AND WHAT CAN BE DONE TO IMPROVE IT (2017);
Louis Hyman, TEMP: HOW AMERICAN WORK, AMERICAN BUSINESS, AND
THE AMERICAN DREAM BECAME TEMPORARY (2018).

2. *See* SANFORD M. JACOBY, EMPLOYING BUREAUCRACY: MANAGERS,
UNIONS, AND THE TRANSFORMATION OF WORK IN AMERICAN INDUSTRY,
1900–1945 (1985).

3. Katharine G. Abraham & Melissa S. Kearney, *Explaining the Decline in
the U.S. Employment-to-Population Ratio: A Review of the Evidence*, 58 J.
ECON. LIT. 585 (2020).

4. *See* ELLEN RUPPEL SHELL, THE JOB: WORK AND ITS FUTURE IN A TIME OF
RADICAL CHANGE 134 (2018).

INDEX

For the benefit of digital users, indexed terms that span two pages (e.g., 52–53) may, on occasion, appear on only one of those pages.